NAXALISM

Myth and Reality

NAXALISM

Myth and Reality

DR. SOHAN RAJ TATER

Foreword by

DR. ANIL DUTTA MISHRA

REGAL PUBLICATIONS

New Delhi - 110 027

NAXALISM
Myth and Reality

ISBN 978-81-8484-139-8

Printed in India at
MAYUR ENTERPRISES
WZ Plot No. 3, Gujjar Market, Tihar Village, New Delhi - 110 018.

Published by
REGAL PUBLICATIONS
F-159, Rajouri Garden, New Delhi - 110 027
Phone : 45546396
E-mail : regalbookspub@yahoo.com

Contents

Dr. ANIL DUTTA MISHRA
Indian Society of Gandhian Studies
Former Secretary General

Rajghat
New Delhi

Foreword

It gives me immense pleasure to write a few lines of appreciation of a very timely book entitled "Naxalism: Myth and Reality" written by an erudite scholar of Contemporary problems, Professor Sohan Raj Tater, former Vice Chancellor of Singhania University, Rajasthan. He has a commendable blending of both Indian Culture and modern knowledge.

Human Development Report, 1990 says that "The real wealth of a nation is its people. And the purpose of development is to create an enabling environment for people to enjoy *long, healthy and creative lives*. This simple but powerful truth is too often forgotten in the pursuit of material and financial wealth". Is human being enjoying a long, healthy and creative lives. If not, who is responsible? The moot question is in development syndrome where are people? And where is protection and care for poor, downtrodden and voiceless people? Uncontrolled Capitalist mode of production and uncontrolled consumerism are the biggest enemy of natural resources which are limited. Industrialism and consumerism and the value systems they promoted, commercialized both nature and human beings. The man became a factor of production, and nature a resource for exploitation. Science and technology have placed enormous power in the hands of man but without a moral code of conduct, its creative potentials have remained dormant. The conflict that is inherent to the man's quest for happiness through material advancement, has taken a variety of forms.

Because in *India we live in three generations* i.e. (a) Village with no electricity and any infrastructure. They still live in inhuman conditions, (b) City with facilities, and (c) Metropolitan cities with all modern facilities.

Naxalism is a developmental issue. It happens when the state run by elites, want to take livelihood of people ruthlessly and unheard their voice. In the developmental process people get alienated and their fundamental rights are taken away by the agent of state. State silences the voice of ignorant, poor and simple people who are the makers of India shining. But government led by irrespective of political parties take away their land, forest, water, culture and everything and leave them at the mercy of corrupt, greedy, unethical people's representatives, Civil servant and repressive machinery of state. Naxalism is nothing but a by product of Capitalist mode of production combined with corruption, unethical practices and corporate greed. Honest politicians, honest bureaucrats and honest person are at back foot. Neither state nor society give them due respect. Result is before us.

Man is by nature a peace loving creature. Man always wants to live in peace and peaceful society. Why peace loving man becomes violent and resorts to violent activities?. One must go in depth. My explanation is when voice of voiceless and powerless goes unheard. Genuine aspirations, of son of the soil, is not fulfilled and in the developmental process they are deprived of land, house, forest and livelihood. Ultimately no option is left but to resort to violent means and become Naxalite or Maoist.

Maoist are poor deprived people. Those who are combating Maoist are also poor people. No rich men send their son or daughter to join military or para-military force. Poor men and women are killing poor men and women. They are same. One is fighting for cause and other is doing professional duty. The elite and capitalist play the game and the sufferer are poor innocent. No one bothers about the fact what will happen when these poor people will understand this truth.

Naxalism/Maoism is a reality in contemporary India. The myth is that very few have understood it properly. I perceive Naxalism/Maoism as an offshoot of failure of developmental paradigm and governmental policies towards people particularly poor and downtrodden. Naxalite/Maoist are not anti national rather anti of capitalistic model of development which deprived them of their land, forest, cuture and livelihood. When neither the local administration nor the State governments and Centre hear and understand their problem, they have no choice but to became Naxlite/Maoist. It is a failure of State and not responding to the root cause of it. In the Naxal/Maoist affected area, the people have not seen the fruit of development. They are living in inhuman condition—no drinking water, no electricity, no hospital, no school etc. In other words, there is absence of basic minimum facilities that is essential for human survival.

Naxalite/Maoist has adopted violence as means to achieve the desire goal is not the right means. They can learn lessions from Srilanka and other countries. Violent means never help to achieve the goal. They should come forward and show the way for future development through constitutional means. Another important aspect is they are killing their own people. Poor is killing poor. Naxalite/Maoist are poor people. From Government side the polish/army man all are poor. The government and Naxalite/Maoist both should give up violent means and come for dialogue. The government must take rapid and massive developmental programmes in entire underdeveloped rural and untouched area of India in a planned manner as a mission. Human beings are basically peace loving people. Government must win the heart of the people and change the chemistry and dynamics of the region. Give the people their due share and self esteem and wipe the tear and remove the fear. Both the side understands their problem from humane perspectives. Even the one step is enough in this direction.

We cannot erect the city of peace on the foundation of violence. If mankind is to live in peace and achieve progress in all spheres, it has to eschew violence and it has to develop a way of life anchored in the philosophy of love and cooperation. We should be cautions of those who want to reach heaven by creating a hell on the earth. It is high time for the individual to change the chemistry of thought and action by adopting Gandhian values in our daily life. We have to start from somewhere to come to overcome the hurdle coming in the way of promoting environmental awareness. In other words, there is a need to reiterate Gandhian values and instead of merely garlanding the portraits of Gandhiji. People must translate his ideals into real life.

We must go back to the spirit and ideals of those halcyon days when we practiced the philosophy of nation first and foremost; when we spoke the language of the heart; when we breathed the air of idealism; when we walked hand in hand on the path of selfless service and sacrifice; when all sons and daughters of the motherland prided themselves in being *"Indian first, Indians last and Indians always"*. The need of the hour is that leaders and people of the country be inspired by the ideals and teachings of Mahatma Gandhi. We need a man of values at the head of a government. We need a philosopher king, whose head is clear and whose heart is in the right place. The policy makers, politicians, intellectuals and scientists must remember in thought and action the Talisman of Mahatma Gandhi:

> "I will give you a Talisman. Whenever you are in doubt, or when the self becomes too much with you, apply the following test.

Recall the face of the poorest and the weakest man whom you may have seen, and ask yourself, if the step you contemplate is going to be of any use to him? Will he gain anything by it? Will it restore him to a control over his own life and destiny? In other words, will it lead to swaraj for the hungry and spiritually starving millions? Then you will find your doubts and yourself melting away."

I hope that this work will be of great help in understanding the problem and placing in correct perspective in solving the problem of Naxalism/Maoism in India.

Anil Dutta Mishra

DR. ANIL DUTTA MISHRA

Preface

In every country, there is an opposition from some peoples, because their needs are not satisfied. But the fact is that in any country a Government can not satisfy all the subjects' needs even in the developed nations also. India is a vast economic country which is having vast value system, struggling to become a developed nation and with this facing internal opposition namly Naxalism. As above said fact, the naxals feel that their needs are not satisfied. Let us see its growth as follows.

The approach to the Naxalites problems needs a blend of firm but sophisticated, handling of naxalites violence with sensitive handling of the developmental aspects. Government can not blame the Naxals, because they are also the subjects of the nation. But their violence is not acceptable by the government. Naxal groups have been raising mainly land and livelihood related issues and they blame the Government settings and Bureaucracy. For a dabate, if a plan or Government establishment are changed in accordance with their likes, then they can not assure that even in those establishment also a naxalism which was handled by them will not rise its head again. Now, India has been facing many challenges like Equality, Jutice (in Social, Economic and Political), Liberty, Fraternity, Peoples' economic development through high economic growth rate and Defence act. These are all the difficult values to be satisfied by India which is a responsive welfare provider. Overcoming and concentrating on the Naxlism gives extra burden to the administration. We spend bulk of money which is the contribution of tax payers (citizens) for the high growth rate in Indian economy and welfare activities, to control the Naxalism through various measures., for example, recent Central Government assistance of Rs. 2475 crors for 55 Naxal affected States and under RSVY (Rashtriya Sram Vikas Yojana) scheme an amount of Rs. 15 crors per year has been given to each of the districts for three years so as to fill in critical gaps in physical and social development in the Naxal affected areas. If controlling the violence and rehabilitating Naxlas would provide for the smooth running of Administration and economic development, then the citizens are resposible to provide for that.

Even though Naxals are claiming about land and livelihood related issues, their attitude is violative. They believe that Administrative and Political institutions are inadequate, espouse local demands, take advantage of the prevelent dissatisfaction and injustice among exploited segment of population and an alternative Government which is promisive to emancipate those people from the clutches of the bureaucrats (in their believe Exploiter) through violation. There are 76 districts and 9 States found to be badly affected by Naxalites. In case, good livelihood, land and wages are properly provided to the peoples living in those areas, then we can avoid them to turn into Naxals and support extremism. Naxals try to sustain their fraternal and logistic links with Nepalese Maoists, though there are no strategic and operational links between them. They often use war like extremism through the armed struggle to capture political power and being Anti-Social and Criminal Element. They are having contemporary weapons. At present, they are attacking simultaneously in large number of targets particularly police forces.

The purpose of this book is to place the material at our place for understanding of Naxalism. I claim no originality. Any error, omission and suggestions for the improvement of the book brought to our notice shall be thankfully acknowledged and incorporated in the next edition.

First of all, I am grateful to Dr. Anil Dutta Mishra a reputed Gandhian Scholar and writer for writing beautiful encouraging

Foreword. From the core of our heart I am grateful to my family members for their moral support which helped us in successful completion of this book on time.

At last, but not the least, I am sincerely thankful to Sh. R.D.S. Bhatia of Regal Publications, for publishing the book in nice form within record time.

SOHAN RAJ TATER

1

The Naxalism : An Introduction

INTRODUCTION

The Naxalites, Naxals or Naksalvadis are a Maoist communist group in India, leaders of the Naxalite-Maoist insurgency. The Naxal name comes from the village of Naxalbari in West Bengal where the movement originated The Naxals are considered far-left radical communists, supportive of Maoist political sentiment and ideology. Their origin can be traced to the split in 1967 of the Communist Party of India (Marxist), leading to the formation of the Communist Party of India (Marxist–Leninist). Initially the movement had its centre in West Bengal. In later years, it spread into less developed areas of rural central and eastern India, such as Chhattisgarh, Orissa and Andhra Pradesh through the activities of underground groups like the Communist Party of India (Maoist).

As of 2009, Naxalites were active across approximately 220 districts in twenty states of India accounting for about 40 percent of India's geographical area, They are especially concentrated in an area known as the "Red Corridor", where they control 92,000 square kilometers. According to India's intelligence agency, the Research and Analysis Wing, 20,000 armed cadre Naxalites were operating in addition to 50,000 regular cadres and their growing influence prompted Indian Prime Minister Manmohan Singh to declare them to be the most serious internal threat to India's national security. The Naxalites are opposed by virtually all other Indian political groups.In February 2009, the Indian Central government announced its plans for broad, co-ordinated operations in all affected states (Chhattisgarh, Orissa, Andhra Pradesh, Maharashtra, Jharkhand, Bihar, Uttar Pradesh, and West Bengal), to plug all possible escape routes of Naxalites.

WHO ARE THE NAXALITES?

The Naxalites are groups involved in violent struggles against landlords, the government and people who, according to them, control all means of production. They believe that only a violent struggle will effectively end the oppression and exploitation of landless workers and tribes and create a classless society. The Naxalites aim to change the face of India, which, in their opinion, cannot be considered free as long as parts of its population are hungry and deprived. The root cause of this, they believe, is the merciless exploitation of the working class by landlords, industrialists and tradesmen. Their fight is not against individuals, but against the entire system. This explains why they target politicians, police officers and government officials. However, critics label them as terrorists who tyrannize people under the pretext of waging a class war. The fact is that Naxality are not terrorists. They are Indian more than the corrupt politicians and bureaucratic who are responsible for social unrest. Naxality are poor people. They are demanding their fundamental rights which is denied by the ruthless state run by corrupt people.

During the Cold War, increasing differences between China and the Soviet Union resulted in a split in the Communist Movement the world over. Out of this split emerged the Naxal movement in India. Ideologically, the Naxalites are followers of Maoism, the basic tenets of which urge the "oppressed classes" to launch a revolution against the "exploiting classes".

In 1967, the Communist Party of India (Marxist) consented to contesting elections and forming a coalition government in West Bengal. Disillusioned by this, a group of party activists, led by Charu Majumdar and Kanu Sanyal, staged a violent uprising against the party leadership. The uprising was triggered off in Naxalbari village in West Bengal when hired goons attacked a tribal who had been granted a piece of land by the court. In retaliation, the local farmers and the rebelling party activists attacked the landlords. The term "Naxal" has its origins in the name of this village. Majumdar, a great fan of Chinese leader Mao Zedong, urged Indian farmers and lower classes to overthrow the government and upper classes whom he held responsible for their plight. His writings were the foundation of Naxal ideology, with the 'Historic Eight Documents' being the cornerstones. In 1967 the Naxalites began breaking away from the mother party, the CPI (M) and established the All India Coordination Committee of Communist Revolutionaries (AICCCR). Two years later, the AICCCR re-emerged as the Communist Party of India (Marxist-Leninist). Today, the CPI (M-L) is the political face of the Naxal Movement in India. The People's War Group and the Maoist Communist Centre are the two principle Naxal organizations that indulge in violent uprisings.

THE NAXAL ZONE OF INFLUENCE

As discussed earlier, the Naxalites portray themselves as representatives of the oppressed people of India, who never get to enjoy the benefits of progress that the rest of the country takes for granted. These groups of people include the Adivasis, Dalits and landless labourers. It comes as no surprise, therefore, that the key areas of Naxal influence include some of the most backward regions of India. The People's War Group's activities extend over Andhra Pradesh, parts of Orissa and the eastern regions of Maharashtra. Bihar, Jharkhand and northern Chhattisgarh are under the influence of the Maoist Communist Centre. These regions have the added advantage of a relatively thick forest cover. The overall inaccessibility of their chosen territories allows the Naxalites to successfully pull off covert operations. Another, rather interesting, fact is that these regions are in the interior parts of the country. One could infer, therefore, that the Naxalites cannot depend on support from outside the country. That they exist in spite of this is testimony to the fact that they enjoy local support. Whether this support comes from a genuine belief in Naxal ideology or out of fear is a matter of debate. The recent success of Maoists in Nepal has emboldened the Naxalites in India. They now feel that if they were to contest elections, they would be able to garner enough votes to seriously influence state politics.

THE STATE vs. THE NAXALITES

- The government has declared the Naxalites as the single biggest internal security challenge ever faced by the country.
- In Chhattisgarh, the government has armed the villagers with guns and other weapons. With the help of paramilitary forces, the villagers have formed a militia to stand up to the Naxalites.
- On the outside, it does look like the government has the interest of the people above everything. But, according to some people, the government's intention is not as noble as it is made out to be. The active confrontation of the Naxalites is actually a bid to gain access to the rich mineral reserves in the forests of the state.
- The government has also, apparently, signed deals with big companies, permitting them to mine the precious ores.
- The Naxalites have actively resisted such industrialisation. The state views this as an attempt to stymie economic growth.

Criticism

Critics claim that the Naxalites have long abandoned their ideology and are nothing more than a group of terrorists now. People who live in regions not under Naxal influence often fail to identify with their ideology and have no trouble justifying the "terrorist" tag. It is believed that the Naxalites extort money from owners of small tracts of land when they cannot do so from the rich landowners. They are also accused of collecting "tax" from the tribals and the poor who they claim to protect. The mass-murder of policemen and government officials has made them unpopular with all political parties. The Naxalites are known to use very brutal methods, including severing of heads, the hacking of limbs and the gouging out of eyes, as they demonstrated in Gadchiroli recently. As protection against the Naxalites' terror tactics, many villagers have formed local armies. In clashes between the Naxalites and these local forces, it is invariably the Adivasis and the poor farmers who suffer the most. The poor people are worst suffer.

The aim of the Naxalites is to establish a communist state in India by the capture of political power through armed struggle. They are for the establishment of a 'people's government' and label the democracy currently existing in the country as 'semi-colonial' and 'semi-feudal', with the ruling classes dominated by neo-imperialists. They point out that democracy in India was not preceded by a democratic revolution, and hence is incomplete at best.

An uprising, a revolution is needed to destroy the old structures of feudal exploitation and class struggle and substitute it with a classless society, where there are no inequalities and political power is in the hands of the masses.

The Naxalites follow the more violent strand of communism, Maoism, which in turn traces itself back to Marxism-Leninism. While concurring with the basic Marxian tenet of the need to replace the old social and economic relations (characterized by owners of capital (the bourgeoisie) using the labour of the working class (proletariat) for its own profit, and where the proletariat is exploited by the bourgeoisie because of the latter's ownership of the means of production), Lenin put forward the idea that there should be a single party which represents the interests of the masses and leads the revolution to overthrow the ruling classes. Leninism also gives the peasantry a position of importance in the revolution because it would be in the Third World countries where the large numbers of peasants would prevent capitalism from becoming a stable force. These basic tenets of Leninism, along with its core Marxian principles laid the base for the dictatorships of Stalin and Mao, marked by massive collectivization experiments where private property was snatched away and all peasant lands were forcibly clubbed together for community farming, leading to deaths in gulags (Soviet prison camps for the dissenters), famines (in China in due to the Great Leap Forward in the 1950s) etc. Following these precepts, the Indian Naxalites too claim to represent a single party with the sole aim of overthrowing the bourgeoisie state and seizing political power.

The other left groups in India do not advocate violence. The Communist Party of India (CPI), which was the parent communist party, broke into two factions after the 1962 Sino-Indian War because of differing interpretations of the War, and its varying implications, especially on the Communist movement in India. While the CPI turned revisionist, moving away from the orthodox Marxian principles and aiming to reinterpret Marxian ideology to suit the Indian situation, the Communist Party of India-Marxist (CPI-Marxist) maintained its allegiance to Soviet and Chinese models of communism. However, it is clear that with the CPI-Marxist's electoral victories (beginning in 1967 in Kerala and West Bengal), it slowly adapted itself to work within the Indian state, preferring to work for a communist cause within a bourgeoisie state than be powerless. They tended to focus on land reforms, reinvigoration of village-level institutions and other pro-poor measures rather than lead a revolution. In fact, the Naxalbari uprising was sought to be crushed by the very government that came to power in West Bengal in 1967, a coalition of the CPI-Marxist and the Congress.

The Naxalites in India are unwilling to enter the political arena in the country since they feel that the state structure is rotten and the Parliament itself has been designed to dupe the masses into believing in a democracy which is dominated by the upper classes. Thus they believe that only a democratic revolution would be able to set up a true democracy, a people's democracy in the country, and they, the CPI-Maoist, are the vanguard of this revolution, as Lenin called the revolutionary party. According to Marx, an essential stage in the transformation of a bourgeoisie, capitalist state to a communist state is 'dictatorship of the proletariat', where the ruling classes will be the workers and the peasants. This would frame policies which would end class struggle (by land redistribution, agrarian reform, promotion of small-scale factories to boost employment etc) and thus pave the way for the utopian communist state, which would effectively end the 'dictatorship of the proletariat' as all would be equal thereon. Lenin called for the revolution and the succeeding dictatorship to be led by a single party (like the Bolsheviks in the Soviet Union, and later, the Communist Party of China in China). Thus the idea of a communist party participating in a multiparty democracy as exists in India was alien to Lenin and Mao. Lenin in fact called it 'parliamentary cretinism' (i.e. parliamentary stupidity). Therefore, following the precepts of their leaders, the Naxalites in India have so far stayed out of the democratic system, preferring 'war' against the Indian state and unwilling to believe that inequalities can be eradicated in a state without a revolution.

In this context, it is interesting to reflect on how the Maoists of Nepal have actively, and successfully, managed the transition from guerilla warfare against the state (represented by the monarchy) to electoral politics. After 10 long years of 'People's War', which saw the deaths of 12000 of its cadre, the Communist Party of Nepal-Maoist finally entered the political arena. While the move may seem as going against the basic tenets of Mao, it was pragmatic and suited the Maoists in Nepal. Party dictatorships have the habit of disintegrating ideologically, and ultimately going against the very people they sought to protect and work in the interests of. The violence which was earlier for the people eventually cuts itself off from their interests and becomes autonomous. This hurts the actual areas of concern, like inequality, hunger, corruption etc. Thus the preference for democracy amongst the masses. Even in India, while the Naxalbari uprising occurred with the implicit consent, and even active participation of, peasants, the recent incidents of violence, such as the Jehanabad jailbreak (2005), the Chhatisgarh attack on police forces (2007) and stray incidents like blasting of train tracks, police stations etc, are increasingly disconnected with the interests of the masses. In this light, it is easy to understand the CPN-Maoist's actions. It undertook violent measures till they had the consent of the majority, and abjured violence when the people's interests (which were favoured by a turn from monarchy towards republican democracy) became antagonistic to further violence. Thus even as ideology calls for dictatorship, the Nepal communists were pragmatic and chose to side with the people, putting the ends on a higher pedestal than the means.

In India on the other hand, the Maoists have not yet followed this direction and continue to advocate violence. However, as these acts of armed uprising against the state become more and more alienated from people interests, the movement may lose popular support. Even as the government follows a policy of 'no negotiation' with the Maoists, instead of undertaking programs to stem the widening disparities which fuel support for them, the cycle of violence can only be expected to grow.

2

Historical Background

The term Naxalites comes from Naxalbari, a small village in West Bengal, where a section of the Communist Party of India (Marxist) (CPM) led by Charu Majumdar, Kanu Sanyal and Jangal Santhal initiated a violent uprising in 1967. On May 18, 1967, the Siliguri Kishan Sabha, of which Jangal was the president, declared their readiness to adopt armed struggle to redistribute land to the landless. The following week, a sharecropper near Naxalbari village was attacked by the landlord's men over a land dispute. On May 24, when a police team arrived to arrest the peasant leaders, they were ambushed by a group of tribals led by Jangal Santhal, and a police inspector was killed in a hail of arrows. This event encouraged many Santhal tribals and other poor people to join the movement and to start attacking local landlords.

Charu Majumdar, inspired by the doctrines of Mao Zedong, provided ideological leadership for the Naxalbari movement, advocating that Indian peasants and lower class tribals overthrow the government and upper classes by force. A large number of urban elites were also attracted to the ideology, which spread through Majumdar's writings, particularly the 'Historic Eight Documents' which formed the basis of Naxalite ideology. In 1967 Naxalites organized the All India Coordination Committee of Communist Revolutionaries (AICCCR), and later broke away from CPM. Violent uprisings were organized in several parts of the country. In 1969 the AICCCR gave birth to the Communist Party of India (Marxist-Leninist) (CPI(ML)).

Practically all Naxalite groups trace their origin to the CPI(ML). A separate offshoot from the beginning was the Maoist Communist Centre, which evolved out of the Dakshin Desh-group. The MCC later fused with the People's War Group to form the Communist Party of India (Maoist). A third offshoot was that of the Andhra revolutionary communists, mainly represented by the UCCRI(ML), following the mass line legacy of T. Nagi Reddy, which broke with the AICCCR at an early stage.

During the 1970s the movement was fragmented into disputing factions. By 1980 it was estimated that around 30 Naxalite groups were active, with a combined membership of 30,000. A 2004 Indian home ministry estimate puts numbers at that time as "9,300 hardcore underground cadre... [holding] around 6,500 regular weapons beside a large number of unlicensed country-made arms". According to Judith Vidal-Hall (2006), "More recent figures put the strength of the movement at 15,000, and claim the guerrillas control an estimated one fifth of India's forests, as well as being active in 160 of the country's 604 administrative districts."India's Research and Analysis Wing, believed in 2006 that 20,000 Naxals were involved in the growing insurgency.

Today some Naxalite groups have become legal organisations participating in parliamentary elections, such as the Communist Party of India (Marxist-Leninist) Liberation. Others, such as the Communist Party of India (Maoist) and the Communist Party of India (Marxist-Leninist) Janashakti, are engaged in armed guerrilla struggles.

On 6 April, 2010 Naxalites launched the biggest assault in the history of the Naxalite movement by killing 76 security personnel. The attack was launched by up to 1000 Naxalites in a well-planned attack, killing an estimated 76 CRPF policemen in two separate ambushes and wounding 50 others, in the jungles of Chattisgarh's Dantewada district. On 17th May naxals blew up a bus on Dantewda-sukhma road in Chhattisgarh, killing 15 policemen and 20 civilians. In third Major attack by Naxals on 29th June, at least 26 personnels of Indian Centre Reserve Forces (CRPF) were killed in Narayanpur district of Chhattisgarh.

The Naxalites gained a strong presence amongst the radical sections of the student movement in Calcutta. Students left school to join the Naxalites. Majumdar, to entice more students into his organisation, declared that revolutionary warfare was to take place not only in the rural areas as before, but everywhere and spontaneously. Thus Majumdar declared an "annihilation line", a dictum that Naxalites should assassinate individual "class enemies" such as landlords, university teachers, police officers, politicians and others.

Throughout Calcutta, schools were shut down. Naxalites took over Jadavpur University and used the machine shop facilities to make pipe guns to attack the police. Their headquarters became Presidency College, Kolkata The Naxalites found supporters among some of the educated elite, and Delhi's prestigious St. Stephen's College, alma mater of many contemporary Indian leaders and thinkers, became a hotbed of Naxalite activities.

The Chief Minister, Siddhartha Shankar Ray, instituted counter-measures against the Naxalites. The West Bengal police fought back to stop the Naxalites. After suffering losses and facing the public rejection of Majumdar's "annihilation line", the Naxalites alleged human rights violations by the West Bengal police, who responded that the state was effectively fighting a civil war and that democratic pleasantries had no place in a war, especially when the opponent did not fight within the norms of democracy and civility.

Large sections of the Naxal movement began to question Majumdar's leadership. In 1971 the CPI(ML) was split, as the Satyanarayan Singh revolted against Majumdar's leadership. In 1972 Majumdar was arrested by the police and died in Alipore Jail. His death accelerated the fragmentation of the movement.

By July 1948, 2,500 villages in the south were organised into 'communes' as part of a peasant movement which came to be known as Telangana Struggle. Simultaneously the famous

Andhra Thesis for the first time demanded that 'Indian revolution' follow the Chinese related stories.

- Naxal plan to kill Dravid, Pawar, Dhoni unearthed path of protracted people's war. In June 1948, a leftist ideological document 'Andhra Letter' laid down a revolutionary strategy based on Mao Tsetung's New Democracy.

1964

CPM splits from united CPI and decides to participate in elections, postponing armed struggle over revolutionary policies to a day when revolutionary situation prevailed in the country.

1965-66

Communist leader Charu Majumdar wrote various articles based on Marx-Lenin-Mao thought during the period, which later came to be known as 'Historic Eight Documents' and formed the basis of naxalite movement.

- First civil liberties organisation was formed with Telugu poet Sri Sri as president following mass arrests of communists during Indo-China war.

1967

CPM participates in polls and forms a coalition United Front government in West Bengal with Bangla Congress. This leads to schism in the party with younger cadres, including the "visionary" Charu Majumdar, accusing CPM of betraying the revolution.

Naxalbari Uprising (25th May): The rebel cadres led by Charu Majumdar launch a peasants' uprising at Naxalbari in Darjeeling district of West Bengal after a tribal youth, who had a judicial order to plough his land, was attacked by "goons" of local landlords on March 2. Tribals retaliated and started forcefully capturing back their lands. The CPI (M)-led United Front government cracked down on the uprising and in 72 days of the "rebellion" a police sub-inspector and nine tribals were killed. The Congress govt at the Centre supported the crackdown. The incident echoed throughout India and naxalism was born.

- The ideology of naxalism soon assumed larger dimension and entire state units of CPI (M) in Uttar Pradesh and Jammu and Kashmir and some sections in Bihar and Andhra Pradesh joined the struggle.

July-Nov: Revolutionary communist organs 'Liberation' and 'Deshbrati' (Bengali) besides 'Lokyudh' (Hindi) were started.

Nov 12-13: Comrades from Tamil Nadu, Kerala, Uttar Pradesh, Bihar, Karnataka, Orissa and West Bengal met and set up All India Coordination Committee of Revolutionaries (AICCR) in the CPI (M).

1968

May 14: AICCR renamed All India Coordination Committee of Communist Revolutionaries (AICCCR) with Comrade S Roy Chowdhury as its convenor. The renamed body decides to boycott elections. Within AICCCR certain fundamental differences lead to the exclusion of a section of Andhra comrades led by Comrade T Nagi Reddy.

1969

April 22: As per the AICCCR's February decision, a new party CPI (ML) was launched on the birth anniversary of Lenin. Charu Majumdar was elected as the Secretary of Central Organising Committee. AICCR dissolved itself.

May 1: Declaration of the party formation by Comrade Kanu Sanyal at a massive meeting on Shahid Minar ground, Calcutta. CPI (M) tries to disrupt the meeting resulting in armed clash between CPI (M) and CPI (ML) cadres for the first time.

- By this time primary guerrilla zone appear at Debra-gopiballavpur (WB), Musal in Bihar, Lakhimpur Kheri in UP and most importantly Srikakulam in Andhra Pradesh.

May 26-27: Andhra police kill Comrade Panchadri

Krishnamurty and six other revolutionaries during a crackdown on Srikakulam struggle in Andhra Pradesh sparking wide protests.

Oct 20: Maoist Communist Centre was formed under Kanhai Chatterjee's leadership. It had supported Naxalbari struggle but did not join CPI (ML) because of some tactical difference and on the question of the method of party formation.

1970

April 27: Premises of Deshabrati Prakashan, which published Liberation and its sister journals, were raided. CPI (ML) goes underground.

May 11: The first CPI (ML) congress is held in Calcutta under strict underground conditions. Comrade Charu Majumdar is elected the party general secretary.

July 10: Comrades Vempatapu Satyanarayana and Adibatla Kailasam, leaders of Srikakulam uprising are killed in police encounter during the crackdown. Comrade Appu, founder of the Party in Tamil Nadu was also killed around September-October. The Srikakulam movement in continued in Andhra Pradesh till 1975.

- Leading lights of literary world of Telugu like Sri Sri, R.V. Shastri, Khtuba Rao, K.V. Ramana Reddy, Cherabanda Raju Varavara Rao, C. Vijaylakshmi with others joined hands to form VIRASAM (Viplava Rachayithala Sangam) or Revolutionary Writers Association (RWA).
- Artistes from Hyderabad inspired by Srikakulam struggle and the songs of Subharao Panigrahi form a group—Art Lovers—comprising the famous film producer Narasinga Rao and the now legendary Gaddar.

1971

In the background of Bangladesh war, the Army tries to crush the ultra-left movement in West Bengal. Uprising in Birbhum marks the high point of this year.

- Art Lovers change its name to Jana Natya Mandali (JNM) late this year. It joins Communists and start propagating revolutionary ideas through its songs, dances and plays. It functioned legally till 1984.

1972

July: Charu Majumdar is arrested in Calcutta on July 16. He dies in Lal Bazar police lock-up on July 28. Revolutionary struggle suffers serious debacle. CPI (ML)'s central authority collapses.

August: 'Pilupu' (The Call), a political magazine was launched in Andhra Pradesh.

- Kondapalli Seetharamaiah reorganises the AP State Committee of Communist Revolutionaries following killing or arrest of the 12-member AP State Committee.

1973

Fresh guerrilla struggles backed by mass activism emerge in parts of central Bihar and Telangana, now a part of Andhra Pradesh.

1974

July 28: The Central Organising Committee of CPI (ML) was reconstituted at Durgapur meeting in West Bengal. Comrade Jauhar (Subrata Dutt) was elected general secretary. Jauhar reorganises CPI (ML) and renames it as CPI (ML) Liberation.

March: Andhra Pradesh Civil Liberties Committee (APCLP) was formed again with Sri Sri as president.

August: Andhra Pradesh state committee was reconstituted with Kondapalli Seetharamaiah representing Telangana region, Appalasuri (coastal AP) and Mahadevan (Rayalseema).

October 12: Radical students union was formed in Andhra Pradesh. It faced brutal suppression but surged again after emergency was lifted.

1975

Following declaration of emergency on June 25 and the

following repression on ultra-leftists and others, the Central Organising Committee in its September meeting decided to withdraw a "common self-critical review" and instead produce a tactical line 'Road to Revolution'. But it did not unity among the cadres. Armed struggles were reported from Bhojpur and Naxalbari.

1976

CPI (ML) holds its second Congress on February 26-27 in the countryside of Gaya, in Bihar. It resolves to continue with armed guerilla struggles and work for an anti-Congress United Front.

1977

Amidst an upsurge of ultra-leftists' armed actions and mass activism, CPI (ML) decides to launch a rectification campaign. The party organisation spreads to AP and Kerala.

February: Revolutionaries organise Telangana Regional Conference in Andhra Pradesh and seeds of a peasant movement are sown in Karimnagar and Adilabad districts of the state. The conference decided to hold political classes to train new cadres and to send "squads" into forest for launching armed struggle. Eight districts of Telangana, excluding Hyderabad, were divided into two regions and two regional committees were elected.

May: Bihar and West Bengal representatives of Central Organising Committee resign at a meeting. Andhra Pradesh representative fails to attend the meet due to the arrest of Kondapalli Seetharamaiah. The Central Organising Committee is dissolved.

1978

Rectification movements (CPI ML and fragments) limits pure military viewpoint and stresses mass peasant struggles to Indianise the Marxism-Leninism and Mao thought.

- CPI (ML) (Unity Organisation) is formed in Bihar under N Prasad's leadership (focusing on Jehanabad-Palamu of Bihar). A peasant organisation—the Mazdoor Kisan Sangram Samiti (MKSS) is formed.

- 'Go To Village Campaigns' are launched by Andhra Pradesh Party of revolutionaries to propagate politics of agrarian revolution and building of Radical Youth League units in Andhra Pradesh villages. It later helped in triggering historic peasant struggles of Karimnagar and Adilabad.

Sept 7: The famous Jagityal march is organised in Andhra Pradesh, in which thousands of people take part.

Oct 20: Andhra Government declares Sarcilla and Jagityal 'disturbed areas' giving police "draconian" powers.

1979

From April to June, Village Campaign was for the first time organised jointly by RSU and RYL in Andhra Pradesh. The two organisations also expressed solidarity with National Movement of Assam.

Between 1979 to 1988, MCC focused on Bihar. A Bihar-Bengal Special Area Committee was established. The Preparatory Committee for Revolutionary Peasant Struggles was formed and soon Revolutionary Peasant Councils emerged. Two founding members of MCC passed away-Amulya Sen in March 1981 and Kanhai Chatterjee in July 1982.

1980

April 22: Kondapalli Seetharamaiah forms the Peoples War Group in Andhra Pradesh. He discards total annihilation of "class enemies" as the only form of struggle and stresses on floating mass organisations.

- Mass peasant movement spreads in Central Bihar.
- CPI (ML) puts forward the idea of broad Democratic Front as the national alternative. It was part of a process to reorganise a centre for All-India revolution after it ceased to exist in 1972.
- The central committee was formed by merging AP and Tamil Nadu State Committees and Maharashtra group of the CPI (ML). Unity Organisation did not join. The tactical adopted by the committee upheld the legacy of Naxalbari while agreeing for rectifying the "left" errors.

- CPI (ML) Red Flag is formed led by K.N. Ramachandran.

1981

CPI (ML) organises a unity meet of 13 Marxist-Leninist factions in a bid to form a single formation to act as the leading core of the proposed Democratic Front. However, the unity moved failed. The M-L movement begins to polarise between the Marxist-Leninist line of CPI (ML) (Liberation) and the line of CPI (ML) (People's War).

- First state level rally is held in Patna under the banner of Bihar Pradesh Kisan Sabha beginning a new phase of mass political activism in the state.

1982

Indian People's Front (IPF) is launched in Delhi at a national conference of CPI (ML) (Liberation). At the end of the year the third Congress of CPI (ML) is organised at Giridih (Bihar), which decides to take part in elections.

1983

Peasant movement in Assam shows signs of revival after allegedly "forced" Assembly elections. IPF plays a crucial role in this regard.

- An all-India dalit conference is held in Amravati (Maharashtra) to facilitate interaction with Ambedkarite groups.

1984

CPI (ML) and other revolutionaries try to woo Sikhs towards joining peasant movement following Operation Bluestar in June and country-wide anti-Sikh riots after Indira Gandhi's assassination in Oct 31 the same year.

1985

People's Democratic Front is launched in Karbi Anglong district of Assam to provide a "revolutionary democratic orientation to the tribal people's aspirations for autonomy".

- PDF wins a seat in Assam Assembly elections bring about the first entry of CPI (ML) cadre in the legislative arena.
- Jan Sanskriti Manch is formed at a conference of cultural activists from Hindi belt at New Delhi.

1986

- Bihar govt bans PWG and MCC

April 5-7: CPI (ML) organises a national women's convention in Calcutta to promote cooperation and critical interaction between communist women's organisations and upcoming feminist and autonomous women's groups.

April 19: More than a dozen "landless labourers" are killed in police firing at Arwal in Jehanabad district of Bihar.

1987

PDF gets transformed into the Autonomous State Demand Committee.

1988

CPI (ML) holds its fourth Congress at Hazaribagh in Bihar from January 1 to 5. The Congress "rectifies" old errors of judgement in the party's assessment of Soviet Union. It reiterates the basic principles of revolutionary communism - defence of Marxism, absolute political independence of the Communist Party and primacy of revolutionary peasant struggles in democratic revolution.

- CPI (ML) ND is formed in Bihar by Comrade Yatendra Kumar.

1989

May: The founding conference of All India Central Council of Trade Union (AICCTU) is held in Madras. Key resolutions are passed at this meet.

November: More than a dozen "left supporters" are shot dead by landlords in Ara Lok Sabha constituency of Bhojpur district in Bihar on the eve of polls.

- CPI (ML) (Liberation) records its first electoral victory under Indian People's Front banner. Ara sends the first "Naxalite" member to Parliament.

1990

In February Assembly election, IPF wins seven seats and finishes second in another fourteen. In Assam too, a four-member ASDC legislators' group enters the Assembly. Special all-India Conference is held in Delhi on July 22-24 to restructure the party.

August 9-11: All India Students Association (AISA) is launched at Allahabad. It opposes VP Singh's implementation of Mandal Commission recommendations.

Oct 8: First all-India IPF rally is held in Delhi. CPI (ML) (Liberation) claims it to be the first-ever massive mobilisation of rural poor in the capital.

- CPI (ML) S R Bhaijee group and CPI (ML) Unity Initiative are formed in Bihar. The former is still active in east and west Champaran.
- Andhra Pradesh Chief Minister Chenna Reddy lifts all curbs on naxal groups. Naxalites operate freely for about a year but observers say it corrupted them and adversely affected the movement.

1991

In the May Lok Sabha elections, Indian People's Front loses Ara seat but CPI (ML) retains its presence in Parliament through ASDC MP.

1992

- Andhra Pradesh bans People's War Group
- CPI(ML) reorganises the erstwhile Janwadi Mazdoor Kisan Samiti in South Bihar as Jharkhand Mazdoor Kisan Samiti (Jhamkis).

May 21: Chief Minister N Janardhan Reddy bans PWG and its seven front organisations again in Andhra Pradesh.

Dec 20-26: CPI (ML) organises its fifth Congress at Calcutta from Dec 20 to 26. CPI (ML) comes out in the open and calls for a Left confederation.

1993

- AISA registers impressive victories in Allahabad, Varanasi and Nainital university elections in Uttar Pradesh besides in the prestigious Jawaharlal Nehru University in New Delhi.
- CPI (ML) launches a new forum for Muslims called 'Inquilabi Muslim Conference' in Bihar.

1994

February: All India Progressive Women's Association is launched at national women's conference at New Delhi.

- Indian People's Front is dissolved and fresh attempts are initiated to forge a united front of various sections of Leftists and Socialists with an anti-imperialist agenda.
- Interactions among various Communists and Left parties intensify in India and abroad to revive the movement drawing lessons from Soviet collapse.

1995

- A six-member CPI (ML) group is formed in Bihar Assembly. Two CPI (ML) nominees win from Siwan indicating the expansion of party's influence in north Bihar.

May: N T Ramarao relaxes ban on Peoples War Group in Andhra Pradesh for three months. PWG goes in for massive recruitment drive in the state.

July: CPI (ML) organises All India Organisation Plenum at Diphu to streamline party's organisational network.

- Revolutionary Youth Association (RYA) is launched as an all-India organisation of the radical youth.

1996

- Five members of ASDC make it to Assam assembly. An ASDC member is re-elected to Lok Sabha. Another ASDC member is elected to Rajya Sabha. ASDC retains its majority in Karbi Anglong District Council and also unseats the Congress in the neighbouring North Cachhar Hills district in Assam.
- CPI(ML) takes initiative to form a Tribal People's Front and then Assam People's Front
- CPI (ML) joins hands with CPI and Marxist Coordination Committee led by Comrade A Roy to strengthen Left movement.
- CPI (ML) initiates the Indian Institute of Marxist Studies. Armed clashes between ultra-leftists and upper caste private armies (like Ranvir Sena) escalate in Bihar.
- The Progressive Organisation of People, affiliated to revolutionary left movement, launches a temple entry movement for lower castes in Gudipadu near Kurnool in Andhra Pradesh. It emerges successful.

1997

CPI (ML) organises a massive 'Halla Bol' rally in Patna. A left supported Bihar bandh is organised as part of "Oust Laloo Campaign" in view of the Rs. 950-crore fodder scam.

1999

- CPI (ML) Party Unity merges with Peoples War.
- Naxalites launch major strikes. CPI (ML) PW kills six in Jehanabad on February 14. MCC kills 34 upper caste in Senai village of Jehanabad.

Dec 2: Three top PWG leaders killed in Andhra Pradesh leading to a large scale brutal naxalite attacks on state forces.

Dec 16: PWG hacks to death Madhya Pradesh Transport Minister Likhiram Kavre in his village in Blalaghat district to avenge the killing of three top PWG leaders in police encounter on Dec 2.

2000

- PWG continues with its revenge attacks. Blasts house of ruling Telugu Desam Party MP G Sukhender Reddy in Nalgonda district in Andhra Pradesh in January. In February it blows up a Madhya Pradesh police vehicle killing 23 cops, including an ASP. It destroys property worth Rs. 5 crore besides killing 10 persons in AP in the same month.

Dec 2: PWG launches People's Guerrilla Army (PGA) to counter security forces offensive.

2001

April: CPI (ML) celebrates 32nd anniversary of its foundation in Patna on April 22 and gives a call to rekindle 'revolutionary spirit of naxalism'.

July: Naxalite groups all over South Asia form a Coordination Committee of Maoist Parties and Organisations of South Asia (CCOMPOSA) which is said to be first such an international coalition. PWG and MCC are part of it.

- As per the Intelligence reports, MCC and PWG establish links with LTTE, Nepali Maoists and Pakistan's Inter-Service Intelligence to receive arms and training. Naxalites bid to carve out a corridor through some areas of Madhya Pradesh, Andhra Pradesh, Bihar, and Uttar Pradesh up to Nepal.

Nov: MCC organises a violent Jharkhand Bandh on Nov 26.

Dec: Naxalites, mainly in AP, Orissa and Bihar celebrate People's Guerilla Week hailing the formation of PGA on Dec 2. The week unfolds major violence in the three states during which a plant of Chief Minister Chandrababu Naidu and the house of an Orissa minister is blown up.

REASONS FOR FAILURE OF NAXALITE MOVEMENT, 1967-75

In a methodical study Dr. Sailen Debnath has surmised the consequences and reasons of failures of the Naxalite Movement organised by Charu Majumdar and Kanu Sanyal. He writes "The Naxalite movement, though continued intensively from 1967 to the middle of 1970s and resurfaced after some years, could not go a long way achieving anything commendable because of the following reasons:

1. The Naxalites wanted to surround the towns and cities by the villages, i.e. they wanted to encircle the urban centres with organized peasant forces of the villages. If the peasant militia could have occupied the cities, according to Majumdar, the so-called bourgeois government would fall making the passage to the coming of a socialist government; but the Naxalites could not and did not come up to a stage capable of organizing the peasants and thereby encircling the towns.
2. Majumdar gave sole importance to secret organization and armed training of its members for the purpose of eliminating the class enemies. As the Naxalites did not have mass level organization, they lacked mass support. Only with select few armed elements not properly educated in political line no big thing could be done.
3. "Khatam" or the action of eliminating the so-called class enemies in villages was a wrong principle of political mobilization by individual murder of select few people whose political class- character was never adjudged by their socio-economic conditions, and the properties they possessed, but very often only by their political affiliation or by the name and colour of the party or parties they directly or indirectly belonged to

for a long or a short period of time. As for example in Jalpaiguri and Alipurduar they killed some petty jotdars who otherwise could have been comrades in action against the capitalists or could be friends in a revolution for radical change.

4. Recruitment in the Naxalite party was never done on proper judgment and scrutiny of the political characters and behaviours of the recruits. It so happened that many people only to feast on their animosities with their personal enemies got recruited in the Naxalite party only to utilize the help of the Naxalites to have their personal enemies in the neighbourhood killed on the basis of pseudo-identification of them as class enemies.
5. In many cases dreaded criminals too enrolled themselves in the Naxalite party with the objective of getting fire arms and to train themselves in the manufacture and use of fire arms. Thus very soon the party turned to be an organization of professional criminal outfits who soon deserted the party after their training period had been over or the cherished objective of owning armaments had been met or realized. Many of these criminals with fire arms soon turned to be dacoits and in many cases they informed the police all about the hidden training centres of the Naxalites and their main purpose in doing so was to have the original Naxalites arrested or else they themselves might fall victims of the Naxalites' targets as approvers in favour of the government..
6. The ruling Congress party inserted their supporters inside the unguarded and porous Naxalite organization for the purpose of knowing and finishing its secret bases and arresting its supporters, and in the same way, the personnels of the government intelligence branch and police too in disguise of Naxalite sympathizers got into the party's inner organization and rounded most of its leaders including Charu Majumdar into the jail. Thus police had information all about the movements of Majumdar after he had gone underground in 1970, and he was

nabbed in Calcutta in July, 1972. The end of his life came in the jail in some days after his arrest; and how he had to pass through the gate of death, most probably in the night of 27th or 28th July, 1972, nobody except the police and the government could know properly, of course, it was told from the side of the government that he died of heart attack.

7. Ordinary people in villages were terrified at the brutal and gruesome ways they killed the fellow villagers vilifying them as class enemies. As for example, at Bholardabri in Alipurduar they killed Rajen Pandit who was a refugee from East Pakistan and arduously was running a family of 12 dependents. By any means he was no class enemy at all. In another case they killed a person, chopped his head off the torso and hanged the head and the torso down the brunches of trees with ropes in two separate places, the horrible sights of which cast a gloom on the faces of bemoaning villagers. Certainly after that they could count no support from the villagers at all.
8. Unbridled repressive measures of the government proved to be more than capable in exterminating the Naxalites in the Districts of Northern Bengal as well as in the whole of West Bengal. Hundreds were slaughtered by the police and paramilitary forces in fake encounters, in jails and in police custody. Many perished because of third degree punishment. The suppression of the Naxalites did not mean to be a heavy task for a government whose objective was to run things smoothly with the help of the British penal code of colonial era under the command of the bureaucrats, police and military who inherited the attitude of their predecessors under the British imperial Government".(Ref. Sailen Debnath, West Bengal in Doldrums, ISBN 9788186860342).

LALGARH VIOLENCE

In late May, 2009 in Lalgarh, West Bengal the Naxalites briefly threw out the local police and staged attacks against the ruling communist government. The region came under assault by Maoist guerrillas. The state government initiated a successfull operation, with central paramilitary forces and state armed police, to retake Lalgarh in early June. Maoist leader Kishenji claimed in an interview that the mass Naxalite movement in Lalgarh in 2009 was aimed at creating a "liberated zone" against "oppression of the establishment Left and its police". He stated this had given the Naxalites a major base in West Bengal for the first time since the Naxalite uprising in the mid-1970s and that "We will have an armed movement going in Calcutta by 2011".

CULTURAL REFERENCES

The British musical group Asian Dub Foundation have a song called "Naxalite", which is featured on the soundtrack to the 1999 film Brokedown Palace. A 2005 movie called Hazaaron Khwaishein Aisi, directed by Sudhir Mishra, was set against the backdrop of the Naxalite movement. In August 2008, Kabeer Kaushik's Chamku, starring Bobby Deol and Priyanka Chopra, explored the story of a boy who is brainwashed to take arms against the state.

In the novel English August by Upamanyu Chatterjee, there is reference to Naxal cadres whom the main protagonist, an IAS officer meets while visiting a tribal village in mid-1980's.

In the novel The God of Small Things by Arundhati Roy, there is a reference to a character joining the Naxalites.

In the little read novel The White Tiger by Aravind Adiga, the Naxals (sic) are mentioned often by the poor and the rich alike.

The 1998 film Haazar chaurasi ki Maa (based on the novel, Hazar Churashir Maa by Mahasweta Devi) starring Jaya Bachchan gives a very sympathetic portrayal of a Naxalbari militant killed by the state. The 2009 Malayalam movie Thalappavu portrays the story of Naxal Varghese, who was shot allegedly dead by the police during the 70s.

The Kannada movie Veerappa Nayaka directed by S. Narayan portrays Vishnuvardhan, a Gandhian whose son becomes a Naxalite. The 2007 Kannada movie Maathaad

Maathaadu Mallige, directed by Nagathihalli Chandrashekhar, again portrays Vishnuvardhan as a Gandhian, who confronts a Naxalite Sudeep and shows him that the ways adopted by Naxals will only lead to violence and will not achieve their objective.

Eka Nakshalwadya Cha Janma, (Marathi: The birth of a Naxal), a novel written by Vilas Balkrishna Manohar, a volunteer with the Lok Biradari Prakalp, is a fictional account of a Madia Gond Juru's unwilling journey of life his metamorphosis from an exploited nameless tribal to a Naxal.

THE NAXALITE PROBLEM IN INDIA

As many as 455 people (255 civilians and 200 security personnel) have been killed in Naxal violence in 2009 (till June-end, and the killings continue), reveal figures released by the Home Ministry. The Naxal-infested States of Chhattisgarh and Jharkhand accounted for 60 per cent of the total deaths in the country in this period. The figures also reveal that Chhattisgarh is the State worst-hit by Naxal violence. In the last three years, the State had topped the list. In 2008, 242 of the total 721 Naxal-related deaths in the country were reported from the State. In 2007, 369 out of 1,565 Naxal-related deaths in the country were reported from Chhattisgarh, and in 2006, 388 out of 678 deaths.

The Naxals, in January-June 2009 period, attacked 56 economic targets. The increasing frequency, with which the Naxals have been hitting economic targets, is alarming. The corresponding figures for the years 2006, 2007, and 2008 were 71, 80, and 109, respectively.

The brazenness with which the Naxals carried out one of their biggest attacks killing at least 36 policemen, including a Superintendent of Police, in Chhattisgarh in second week of July 2009, has left the security establishment shaken. Prime Minister Manmohan Singh has described the Naxalite problem as 'the single largest threat to India'.

The CPI (Maoist) swells the list of indigenous terror groups operating in India to 27, making India home to the largest number of domestic terrorist organisations in the world. In June 2009, the Ministry of Home Affairs (MHA) named the CPI

(Maoist) as 34th terrorist organisation under the Unlawful Activities (Prevention) Act; seven of these are transnational terror groups.

CPI (Maoist) join ranks with ULFA and SIMI, and lesser known entities such as Hynniewtrep National Liberation Council of Meghalaya, Kanglei Yaol Kanba Lup of Manipur and Akhil Bharat Nepali Ekta Samaj, which though virtually unheard of are considered deadly enough by the government to be designated as terrorist organisations.

Of the seven transnational terror groups, only two—al-Qaida and LTTE—are truly global names. The other five are: Lashkar-e-Taiba (LeT), Harkatul Mujahideen, Al Badr, Jamat-ul-Mujahid and Hizbul Mujahideen (HM), which are all Pakistan based terror outfits fighting Indian security forces in Kashmir.

Amongst developed countries, only UK has a significant number of terror groups breeding close to home in form of nine Irish militias such as the Ulster Freedom Fighters and the Irish Republican Army.

The 'Red terror' spots have begun to pop up in India's capital and northern States' forest and hilly areas too. It seems that the Maoists are interested in enlarging their area of influence outside the jungles of the 'Red Corridor' that runs from the Nepal border down to Andhra Pradesh. Lately, they have begun targeting India's seat of power—New Delhi—and many other cities by setting up urban bases with the aim to penetrate and influence policy makers, judiciary, media, civil liberty, human rights, cultural, Dalit, women and youth organisations. So far, the urban units are not indulging in violence. But who knows when they may start firing guns.

Seized documents of the CPI (Maoist) Politburo and Central Committee talk about the need to run a secret service and unleash psychological wars through effective networking of various friendly groups in the urban areas.

According to a confidential report of the military intelligence, India's 231 districts in 13 States, including three in the NCR, are now being targeted by the Maoists to achieve their ultimate aim—seize power in Delhi by 2050.

So far, it is believed that about 170 districts falling under the dreaded 'Red Corridor', also known as the Dandekaran Belt, are reeling under the Maoist terror. In Chhattisgarh, Bastar's dense jungles are considered to be the Maoists' centre of gravity. In southern Bastar, the Maoists have declared the Chintainer area as their Dandekaran State's capital.

The 'Red Corridor' runs through the dense forest and tribal belt, from Nepal through Bihar, Jharkhand, Orissa, Chhattisgarh, Madhya Pradesh and all the way to Andhra Pradesh and to the upper reaches of Maharashtra, and some parts of Karnataka. Inside their corridor, the Naxalites run a parallel government and vow to continue their fight against the state—a full-fledged war they call 'people's struggle'.

All the Left-wing militant organisations, including the Maoist Communist Centre (MCC) and the People's War Group (PWG), after their merger are now operating under the flagship rebel party—CPI (Maoist).

The Central intelligence reports have also issued a warning that the Maoists are now in the process of identifying 'new operational areas' across the country. They are keenly looking at industrial belts, where big corporate houses are planning to set up the Special Economic Zones (SEZs), an easy target to launch violent agitation.

The Central Committee of the CPI (Maoist) has published a secret red book 'Strategy and Tactics of the Indian Revolution', which is said to be the Naxals' Bible. The book says: "The central task of the revolution is seizure of political power through protracted People's war." Talking about supporting sub-national movements in India, the book says: "Lakhs of enemy's armed troops have been deployed since long in J&K and the north-eastern States. More and more nationalities may come into armed confrontation with the reactionary Indian State, so it will be difficult for the Indian ruling classes to mobilise all their armed forces against our revolutionary war." It further says the urban areas are one of the main sources which provide cadre and leadership having various types of capabilities essential for People's war.

3

The Origins and the Ideology of the Naxalite

INTRODUCTION

The history of Naxalism in India is described by Sumanta Banerjee, its most respected chronicler, as 'tortuous'. A complicated diagram in Bela Bhatia's study of 'The Naxalite Movement in Central Bihar'24 shows how very fragmented the Movement became before the merger of the two principal groups, the Communist Party of India (Marxist-Leninist) [CPI(M-L) People's War] and the Maoist Communist Centre of India (MCCI) in 2004.25 In 1995-96, Bhatia reports, there were as many as 17 different active groups in Bihar. Of these groups, the three most significant were: 'Liberation', by that time following the line of participation in parliamentary politics, and recognised by the Election Commissioner as the 'CPI(ML)'; the Maoist Communist Centre, considered to be 'extreme left'; and 'Party Unity' which stood somewhere in-between. What follows, therefore, is the merest sketch of a complex history.

Drawing on a longer history of Communist-led armed struggle by peasants against landlords, moneylenders and government officials—especially that in Telengana between 1946 and 1951—Naxalism has its immediate origins in the debates within the Indian communist movement of the 1960s about the 'correct' strategic line to be taken in order to establish communism in India's particular circumstances. The Movement took off in May 1967 and is named after a village in the far north of West Bengal where a group of revolutionaries—who repudiated the approaches of the major communist parties as 'reformist'—launched an armed uprising of peasants against local landlords. It spread quite quickly into parts of Bihar, Srikakulam District of Andhra Pradesh, Koraput in Orissa and some other areas where guerilla squads of poor and landless peasants drove out landlords. In many cases, however, action degenerated into indiscriminate violence following the injunction of Charu Mazumdar who had emerged as the Movement's leader to undertake 'annihilation of class enemies'. Mazumdar once wrote that the battle-cry of the movement should be: 'He who has not dipped his hand in the blood of class enemies can hardly be called a communist'. Dilip Simeon argues of this that, 'What stands out is the freedom accorded to "petty-bourgeois intellectual comrades" to instigate the murder of anyone they deemed a class enemy', the legitimacy of this being seen as self-evident and derived from 'the assumed superiority of the party's version of Marxism-Leninism'.

Further he argues that the Maoist/Naxalite Movement has been intellectually driven from its origins, led by middle-class ideologues who take it upon themselves to lead 'the people' and who claim 'correct knowledge' for themselves. Aditya Nigam argues similarly:

> The adivasis cannot represent themselves; they must be represented, it would seem. They must be represented either by agents of the state... or by the revolutionaries... (and)... the voice of the revolutionary is almost always that of a Brahman/upper caste Ganapathy or Koteswara Rao or their intellectual spokespersons. So we have a Maoist-aligned intelligentsia vicariously playing out their revolutionary fantasies through the lives of adivasis, while the people actually dying in battle are almost all adivasis.

The truth claims made by the Maoist leaders are inherently linked, Dilip Simeon argues to their attachment to armed struggle. This attachment is 'the product of a correct theory' to which party cadres have privileged access. Ultimately, it is struggle for the classless society that defines what is right but the result of this way of thinking is that 'the defining feature of the Maoist agenda' has become 'an insistence on killing'. As discussed below, Maoists now strenuously defend themselves against this argument, claiming that 'Annihilation is the last choice'.

Naxalism in the early 1970s met with matching violence from the state and it appeared to have been very largely overcome, even before Mrs Indira Gandhi's Emergency stifled opposition.

General Secretary Ganapathy says that two parties, the CPI(M-L) and the Maoist Communist Centre (MCC) were both formed in 1969 and 'failed to form a unified Maoist party at that juncture'. He also says that the party [he seems to refer to the CPI(M-L)] had already started to disintegrate into several groupings by 1971.32 One group, Liberation, later decided to organise mass fronts and eventually participated in parliamentary politics. By the time when Charu Mazumdar died in police custody in 1972, the 'revolution' appeared to be over. The revolutionary movement has, however, risen again and again because the factors that lend it credence and give it life persist—most importantly the continuing denial of justice and human dignity to Dalits and tribals across the country.

The line of the Movement set out in the 1970 Programme of the CPI (M-L), and largely repeated in that of its eventual successor the CPI (Maoist) in 2004, adopts Mao's view that in semi-feudal and semi-colonial countries like India 'under the neo-colonial form of imperialist indirect rule', the immediate task of the communist party is to organise landless labourers, poor peasants and exploited middle peasants in armed struggle against their oppressors. The aim is to foster a democratic revolution:

> Whose axis and content is agrarian revolution, rejects the parliamentary path of participation in elections, and pursues the main objective... (of liberating)... the rural

> areas first and then having expanded the base areas—the centre of democratic power in rural areas—advance towards countrywide victory through encircling and capturing the cities.

In the 1980s, which is the second phase in the history of the Movement as conceptualised by Sumanta Banerjee, rethinking took place on the part of some survivors of the first phase who favoured participation in parliamentary politics and trade union activities. Others stuck with the line of armed struggle whilst also encouraging mass mobilisation through the setting up of open fronts. By the end of the decade groups following the latter course, including CPI(M-L) Party Unity in Bihar, and People's War Group [CPI(M-L) People's War Group] in Andhra Pradesh had built strong bases in parts of these two states and others in Madhya Pradesh, Maharashtra and Orissa. It has been from these areas that the Maoists have succeeded over the last twenty years, in spite of both state repression and resistance against them carried on by the militias of dominant groups, in building the 'red corridor' stretching from the upper Gangetic plain bordering Nepal across plains and through the forested hills that parallel the East Coast of India down as far as northern Tamil Nadu. The corridor is twice the geographical size of the other two insurgency-affected areas of India, in the North East and Kashmir. The Maoists are now believed to operate in over a third of India's districts.

The Movement is currently, Banerjee thinks, in its third phase following the agreement of leaders and cadres of scattered and divided groups to the creation of the single revolutionary party, the CPI(Maoist) in 2004. The reasons for 'fusion' after decades of fragmentation in the Movement are unclear. Nonetheless, it is reasonable to suppose that the Indian activists have been influenced by the example of the Nepali Maoists—even though they may also be critical of the latter for having agreed to join the electoral process. It is probably no accident that the merger in 2004 was partly facilitated by the Nepali leader, Prachanda. Whatever the factors behind the fusion that has taken place, it appears to have brought about a significant regeneration of the Movement, having 'given synergy to the new outfit in terms of strength, capability and resources—for launching attacks on the security forces'. This fusion has also provided a large swathe of the country within which the Maoists are able to move without the problems of coordination that afflict the state police forces. Both the scale and frequency of incidents in which the Maoists have confronted the security forces have increased, culminating most recently in the attack on 6 April 2010 in a forest in eastern Chhattisgarh that left 78 armed policemen dead. This occurred not long after an attack on a police camp at Silda in West Bengal in which 24 policemen were killed.

The CPI(Maoist), as pointed out earlier, has reaffirmed the programmatic line of the CPI(M-L) of 1970, committing to a people's war for seizure of power whilst also stating that it will wage struggles against the Government of India's plans to set up Special Economic Zones and against the displacement of tribals and forest dwellers by mining and other projects. I was informed in March 2010 by the noted human rights activist, Professor G. Haragopal of the University of Hyderabad, that the Maoists are now prioritising mobilisation, especially of tribals against mining and other projects involving displacements of people. Their prime objective has become that of mobilisation against 'imperialism' as reflected in India's economic liberalisation and the effects of globalisation rather than 'anti-feudal' struggles.

Another human rights activist, K. Balagopal, provides an illuminating history of the Movement in Andhra Pradesh. In the 1970s, the Naxalites fought fairly successfully, in spite of police actions against landlordism (including the practice of begar or bonded labour) and then encouraged tribals to cut down reserve forests for cultivation. This was by 'far and away the most successful land struggles of the Naxalites' until later in the mid-1990s changing their policy in the light of changed circumstances, they imposed 'quite a successful ban on the cutting of forests'. In the early period, in the northern Telengana region of Andhra Pradesh, Balagopal says, the Naxalites spread mainly through mass organisations of agricultural labourers, students and youth, but thereafter in this region and elsewhere in the state, heavy repression on the part of government forces brought an increased reliance on armed squads:

> The immediate economic and social problems of the masses took a back seat and the battle for supremacy with the state became the central instance of struggle. . . . This requires a range of acts of violence, which have no direct relation to the immediate realisation of any rights for the masses, though the resulting repression invariably hits at the masses.

Unsurprisingly, this has led to questioning amongst people as to whether they have not been made into 'guinea pigs of revolution'. New generations, though they may have benefited from the earlier actions of the Maoists, are less sympathetic to them than were people of their parents' generation, while at the same time the tactics employed by the state in Andhra have seriously weakened them. These tactics included the creation of special police forces—the 'Greyhounds'—that live and operate like the Naxalites' own squads and are 'bound by no known law, including the Constitution of India'. 'Today, the state stands as the best example of the success of counter-revolutionary strategies of a government'. The Movement in Andhra Pradesh has, however, supplied leaders more widely as in Bastar, in neighbouring Chhattisgarh and nationally. Kishenji, for example a politburo member, is from Karimnagar. The Andhra experience, of the shift from mass mobilisation to armed struggle and from tactics that address people's everyday problems to the remote goal of seizing state power triggered by the proscribing of the mass movements by the state is one that has been repeated more widely—and increasingly so. The CPI(Maoist) was formally banned by the Government of India as a terrorist organisation under Section 41 of the Unlawful Activities (Prevention) Act on 22 June 2009. It had previously been declared an 'unlawful association' by a number of states, including Andhra Pradesh.

THE NAXALITES'/MAOISTS' PROGRAMME

The programme of the CPI(Maoist), once the new people's democratic state is established, however, is one with which 'a large chunk of the Indian political class should have nothing to quarrel about'. The party proposes to redistribute land to poor peasants and landless labourers according to the slogan 'land to the tillers'; to ensure the land rights of women; 'to ensure all facilities for the growth of agriculture', including ensuring 'remunerative prices' for agricultural products'; to regulate working conditions and ensure that wages are adequate and equal between the sexes; to guarantee the right to work and 'improved living conditions for the people'; and 'to move towards the elimination of regional imbalances'. Much of this also appears in the Common Minimum Programme with which the United Progressive Alliance (UPA), headed by the Congress Party, set out (also in 2004), while the major established party of the Left, the CPI(M), remains committed to the abolition of landlordism and radical land reforms. Contrary to what is suggested by some commentators, the CPI(Maoist) does have a coherent programme.

The Maoists are not just armed bandits, as they are sometimes represented as being (as in the Frontline report from Lalgarh) and in spite of the history of attachment to violence that Simeon critiques in the Seminar article referred to earlier. They are now seen increasingly as being more or less exclusively an armed movement with no concern for mass mobilisation has come about because state action against them leaves them with little scope for the latter, which has tended to shrink (as we saw from Balagopal's account from Andhra Pradesh outlined earlier)—or at least apparently so (close observers like Navlakha report that organising goes on wherever it is possible for the Party to do so).

The chances of land reform being carried out in India by intervention from above now seem remote. Neither is there significant pressure for such reforms from below in the major agricultural regions of the country. Moreover, the major left parties have chosen not to concentrate attention on marginal areas where the land issue still is alive. The Maoist/Naxalite organisations have filled the gap and Gupta argues that 'the major Naxalite contribution to Indian politics is that they have kept alive the agrarian demands of the rural poor through persistent but not always successful struggles'. Their emphasis, too, on armed resistance to oppression by bigger landowners and rich farmers who often still subject Dalits and adivasis to everyday humiliation has appeal to many of these historically oppressed people. Gupta thinks that it has a large mass following because 'no other political party in the country has taken up the cause of the rural poor with such single-minded zeal and devotion'. He thinks this even though he questions the priority that the Maoists themselves seem to give to the path of armed revolution, reinforcing the impression that theirs is a guerilla formation rather than a political party. Gupta also believes that their strategic-tactical line is quite inadequate in the context of present day India—as he says, most of India is not Dandekaranya (one of the major tribal-occupied forest areas of Chhattisgarh). Balagopal, similarly, has argued that 'the main reason for the wide popularity of the Naxalites in the entire forest region abutting the Godaveri river in Telengana, Vidarbha and Chhattisgarh is the protection they gave to the forest dwellers for cultivation in reserve forests, the substantial increase they achieved in the payment for picking tendu leaf and the end they put to the oppressive domination of the headmen and patwaris'. The massive transfers of forest and agricultural land for infrastructural, mining and industrial projects that are either planned or are now taking place will lend even greater strength to the Naxalites.

TACTICS, MOBILISATIONS AND PATTERNS OF SUPPORT

The few ethnographic studies are strongly confirm these general arguments about the extent to which the Naxalites win support amongst, and articulate the needs and aspirations of poor and landless peasants and adivasis, and perhaps especially of young men and women amongst these groups. This is so even if they actually enter a region through the rural middle class of upper caste elites and educated well-to-do adivasis, as has been the case in the part of Jharkhand studied by Alpa Shah. These studies also, however, highlight the tensions and contradictions in the tactics and actions of the movements. The relationship between the mainly urban, educated middle class leadership and the peasantry is fraught with tensions. There are contradictions between the immediate tactics of the groups, of opposing the dominant landowners, redistributing land, raising wages and generally of changing rural power relations, all of which answers to the problems that their supporters confront and on the other hand, their longer run goals of establishing socialism through the take-over of state power. It seems from the ethnographies that, unsurprisingly, the extent to which the leadership has been able to develop a 'revolutionary consciousness' amongst the poor peasantry is very limited. George Kunnath's research in particular, shows how support amongst Dalits for the Maoists in Central Bihar weakened considerably, as the latter sought to bring in men from the middle and upper castes in pursuit of the goal of capturing state power and rewarded the higher caste members of their armed squads (dastas) more highly than the Dalits. The tendency on the part of the leadership to romanticise the revolutionary character of the peasantry is sometimes a problem and it is clear that such as this consciousness is, it may well be suppressed when government provides adequately for the most immediate needs of the people. The other big tension is between mass mobilisation and the necessarily secretive, armed power of the underground movement which is not inherently democratic at all. This relates in turn to the contradiction between the moral basis of the Maoist movement and the violence that it perpetrates. Violence can undermine that moral base and alienate supporters as has happened, according to Balagopal's account—summarised earlier—in Andhra Pradesh. The understandable sense of their persecution amongst Maoist cadres, confronted by the violence of the state, may lead to the indiscriminate use of force and their alienation from the people they claim to fight for. It is clear, too, and also unsurprising that there is but a thin line between the 'revolutionary' and the criminal thug. One of the early leaders in Central Bihar (one of a pair referred to colloquially as 'Marx and Engels') was a Yadav dacoit who had served a long prison sentence for the murder of a police constable.

Bhatia and Kunnath provide ethnographic evidence that the social base of the Movement in Central Bihar, when the Movement was strong there, was amongst the landless, small and marginal peasants of lower and intermediate castes, though there were some supporters from amongst higher castes and classes and whose presence was felt in the leadership. These authors show that there was a perception amongst poorer people that Naxalites were 'good people', who were opposed to their oppressors and who supported them in a struggle for their basic rights. But according to Bhatia, people understood the objective of the movement as being 'change', not 'revolution'. They supported it because they felt that the Naxalites shared their sense of injustice rather than for any ideological reasons. The appeal of 'class struggle' was as a means of securing needs for higher wages, land redistribution and freedom from harassment. Bhatia notes that people petitioned the Maoists for exactly the same things for which they also petitioned government.

Bhatia describes mobilisations by Dalits against Bhumihar landowners in Bhojpur; Kunnath the struggles between Maoist-led landless Dalits and Kurmi landholders in another village in Central Bihar. In both cases, the accounts show that the 'feudal' power of the landowners was undermined but at a high cost in terms of human life. In this region, of course, the Maoists began to be opposed in the 1990s by vigilante gangs set up by the landowners, like the Bhumihars' Ranbeer Sena. Still, the ethnographies show that the Maoist mobilisations delivered some real benefits to landless peasants. They established land rights for some, raised wages in the areas of struggle and perhaps above all, inspired poor people to assert themselves as human beings and to claim their social and political rights. 'Honour' or 'self-respect' (izzat) appears for many to have been their most important achievement from their participation in the mass mobilisations of the Maoists.

In practice, Bhatia argues on the basis of extensive fieldwork in Central Bihar in the mid-1990s, a large part of the Movement's activities were non-violent (demonstrations, dharnas and the like). Still, there were significant differences between Liberation (castigated by General Secretary Ganapathy as having degenerated 'after a history of glorious struggle'), Party Unity and the MCC over the extent of their commitment to the mass line represented by the open fronts set up by the various groups. Liberation formed the Indian People's Front (IPF) and the Bihar Pradesh Kisan Sabha (BPKS) in the early 1980s and both flourished. Party Unity set up the Mazdoor Kisan Sangram Samiti (MKSS) was banned in 1986 but was later renamed Mazdoor Kisan Sangram Parishad (MKSP). But underground, armed action was always important. At the outset and again more recently according to other commentators, the groups relied almost exclusively on armed tactics. These were undertaken by the dasta (squads), each with 6-10 members recruited mostly locally from amongst the labouring classes, though they might also include middle class members, some from outside the area. The most important role of the dasta, according to Bhatia, was (in the 1990s) to protect the open fronts; open fronts and underground groups were intimately linked. Kunnath records that they were referred to always together as the sanghathan. His account, from fieldwork undertaken more recently than Bhatia's, shows that the squads increasingly included middle class and middle caste members as the Maoists sought to build a wider cross-class movement in the pursuit of the goal of securing state power. His friend Rajubhai, a landless Dalit who had been the leader of a dasta and who appears to be an organic intellectual, told him that:

> When the sanghathan came here, it began among the mazdoor varg (working class). The cadres used to sleep and eat in the mud houses of the mazdoor. It fought for the issues of the working classes—land and wages, as well as against social abuses, exploitation and sexual abuse of women. But now that the sanghathan has got a foothold here, its ambition has grown into one of capturing state power. So they have started taking in people from dominant castes, against whom we fought previously. As a result of the entry of the landowning castes into the sanghathan, it is hesitant to raise the issues of land and wages. For the last twenty years, wages have remained the same: three kilos of paddy for a day's work. The working class is no longer a priority for the sanghathan.

Rajubhai's disaffection from the sanghathan was completed by the fact that landless Dalits in the dastas, though they were the ones who died or suffered physically the most, were actually paid less than were the middle caste members. This appears to be a rather shocking denial of the moral claims of the Movement.

A village study from South Bihar by Shashi Bhushan Singh presents a more complex, even confusing picture, though it also bears out some of the points made by Bhatia and Kunnath. Here it appears that the IPF, the open front of Liberation and the MKSS of Party Unity—though they were both led locally mainly by Yadavs—were a source of support for Dalits in their struggles against higher castes for higher wages and for their dignity. Singh says, 'The biggest contribution of the Naxalites towards the empowerment of the poor has been the taming of the upper castes'. These struggles took place, however, in a context in which the traditional dominance of Rajputs had already been weakened by the effects of economic development. This, in various ways, drew people increasingly out of the village. By the later 1990s, Dalit support for the Naxalites was apparently waning, mainly because of the improvements that had taken place in the Dalits' economic condition and perhaps also because the class contradiction between the landed and landless had by then become less clear-cut: 'The importance of land as a factor of livelihood and dominance is decreasing . . . [as] . . . the locus of the economy has partially shifted away from the village'. The politics of Maoism in this case were greatly influenced by caste and its implications for the wider political realignments that took place in Bihar in the 1990s. The Dalits themselves were divided by class differences (mainly between the Chamars and the rest); many of the Yadavs shifted politically to become supporters of Lalu Prasad Yadav's Rashtriya Janata Dal (RJD); while the MCC had entered the region later than the other groups and through upper caste Bhumihars and Rajputs, and finally became closely associated with the latter when the Bhumihars opposed to Lalu and the RJD; also shifted to become the main opposition to the Maoists through the Ranbeer Sena. In this case, 'The MCC supported Rajputs and opposed the Scheduled Castes initially in order to gain supremacy vis-à-vis the MKSS and later for survival vis-à-vis the police and Ranvir Sena. An organisation formed to support the Scheduled Castes ended up by supporting the dominant castes'. The neatness of class conflict is completely upset in this case—and no doubt, the same is true of many other areas.

While it may be true, as it is according to the close observers of the Movement in Central Bihar whose work has been referred to here, that revolutionary violence can appeal to these who have been subjected to violence by their social 'superiors' over generations, Bhatia particularly—like Banerjee—is clearly deeply concerned about the way in which violence corrupts the Movement. Her conclusion—with which, I believe, Kunnath's arguments are in sympathy—is worth quoting in full:

> The Naxalite movement will thrive only to the extent that its vision resonates with the people. The wider the gap between the two, the higher the chances the movement will fizzle out. The present formula is a mélange of convenience between the leaders who dream of Maoist revolution and people who aspire for practical change. In order to bring about a genuine people's movement, the Naxalite leaders have to be ready to walk at the pace of the people and let their concerns guide the vision of the movement.

The story of the Movement in Andhra Pradesh according to Balagopal, as recounted earlier, is salutary. There, he argues, the gap between the visions of leadership and masses has seriously weakened the Movement. The leadership has the commitment to 'armed struggle' that is explained in the Party Programme, while the Maoists are also subjected to such violence by the state that both sides have become locked into armed conflict. Then the experiences, for notable example, of the attempts in Andhra Pradesh to reach a negotiated settlement have shown just how difficult this is to achieve given the legitimate suspicions of the Maoists of the government and vice versa.

Thus far there are no ethnographic studies of the Movement in the Bastar region of Chhattisgarh to compare with those for Central Bihar, though Nandini Sundar who has carried on substantial ethnographic research in the region—if not in the Maoist dominated areas, as she says—has written on it, drawing on interviews conducted as part of a Citizens' Initiative visit there in May 2006. Her information about the activities of Salwa Judum is substantiated by interviews and observations in the field reported by Jason Miklian. Sundar records that the Maoists 'claim to include 60 lakh (6,000,000) people in the "organisational sweep" of their Dandakaranya "guerilla zone"', where they have established mass organisations—the most important of which are the Dandakaranya Adivasi Kisan Mazdoor Sanghathan (DAKMS) and the Krantikari Adivasi Mahila Sanghathan (KAMS)—that are colloquially called sanghams. The Maoists claim, also, to have carried on a great deal of developmental work, including the establishment of 135 people's clinics, educational facilities and a large number of minor irrigation works. Sundar comments that while these efforts—assuming that the Maoists' claims are accurate—are not equivalent to what the government might have achieved, they do show much greater commitment to people's development. The KAMS is said to have taken up women's issues and the Maoists have consciously promoted Gondi language and literature.

These positive efforts, however, are compromised by other Maoist activities when they have 'resisted even genuine government initiatives'. For example, 'While recognising that traders cheat adivasis over minor forest produce, (the Maoists) have defended them against government attempts to introduce cooperatives to buy tamarind and tendu'. Miklian, too, comments that most villagers 'are upset at Naxal opposition to government programmes and efforts to block participatory elections'. More significant still, than this, has been the 'brute force' that has accompanied their work. Sundar argues, 'Their supporters need to debate whether armed struggle was necessary to their positive work and whether peaceful mass mobilisation would not work better. Certainly, the attempt to defend their guerilla zone seems now to have overtaken people's needs. . . .'. Her conclusion then is exactly like Bhatia's from Bihar or Balagopal's from Andhra. Gautam Navlakha gives a somewhat more sympathetic account of the Maoists in Bastar from the journey he made in their 'base area' there, where they run their Jantanam Sarkar or 'people's government' in January 2010. He, like Arundathi Roy, was evidently very impressed by the self-discipline of the young cadres amongst whom he observed remarkable gender equality. He notes the large numbers of women and that many platoons of the

People's Liberation Guerilla Army have women commanders. He says 'It is significant that women comprise by far and away the most articulate members of the movement' and records its work to encourage (not 'decree') the emancipation of women as also to develop education, healthcare and agricultural production. According to Navlakha's account, the Maoists are very concerned indeed to explain and defend their policy in regard to violence. They point to the violence that is carried on against the people quite routinely by police and private militia of the Salwa Judum and strongly assert that only 'enemies of the people' were killed by them. This defence was also articulated forcefully by General Secretary Ganapathy in his interview with Myrdal and Navlakha, and by the Jharkhand leader Gopalji, interviewed by Alpa Shah. But it is clear that there is a great deal of sensitivity amongst the Maoist leadership about undisciplined violence. Navlakha says, 'I pointed out that each time the party committed a mistake and apologised, it could not help advance the movement forward. Did not this raise issues about discipline?' This line of questioning clearly discomfited those with whom he spoke. There can be no doubt that there is a spiral of violence as Bhatia and others show. At the same time, the police who are set against the Maoists come from what Human Rights Watch has described as a 'broken system':

> 'A dangerous anachronism, the police have largely failed to evolve from the rulersupportive, repressive forces they were designed to be under Britain's colonial rule. . . . Instead of policing through public consent and participation, the police use abuse and threats as a primary crime investigation and law enforcement tactic. The institutional culture of police practically discourages officers from acting otherwise, failing to give them the resources, training, ethical environment and encouragement to develop professional police tactics. Many officers even told Human Rights Watch that they were ordered or expected to commit abuses'.

There are some other points that emerge from the few ethnographies. One interesting finding is that of Amit Desai from his fieldwork in one of the two Naxalite affected districts of Maharashtra. Here the presence of the Maoists has had the effect of bringing the police, moved into 'advanced bases', closer to village people. Aware as they now are of the need to 'win hearts and minds', the police sometimes provide support for villagers in their interactions with other bodies of the state. But they are also convinced that 'social backwardness' is a major reason why people may support the Maoists. With this mindset, the police have attempted at a kind of social reform by trying to regulate local religious practice and such activities as witch-detecting and ghost-finding. This has had the consequence, in this case, of pushing people into closer involvement with the alternative religious practice offered by a particular Hindu sect that is aligned with the Hindu right. The Maoists have generally been silent in regard to the increasing influence that Hindu nationalists have sought to build amongst tribals. Sumanta Banerjee writes that 'their major failure has been their powerlessness in putting up an effective resistance to the Hindu religious fascist forces which have imposed a reign of terror over members of the Muslim and Christian religious minorities. The indifference of the Maoist leaders to these major flashpoints of popular grievances and resistance indicates to some extent the alienation they are prone to'.

RESPONSES OF STATE, THE ROLE OF CAPITAL, AND 'DURABLE DISORDER'

Here I discuss, in particular, the responses of the state to the Maoists in Chhattisgarh though I believe the key points made are ones that are of general significance. The efforts made by the Government of Chhattisgarh to tackle the Naxalites/ Maoists in the state, until 2005, had proven largely ineffectual. It was said by Ajai Sahni, Executive Director of the Institute of Conflict Management, Delhi, 'Chhattisgarh forces still lag behind other Indian states in both quantitative and qualitative terms'. It has been in this context that the policy of recruiting 'Special Police Officers' from amongst local people was adopted by the Central Reserve Police Force in 2006 as a way of increasing manpower cheaply. Sundar records that many of those recruited were minors and they and others 'were attracted by the promise of Rs. 1,500 per month, the machismo of weapons and the hope of getting permanent employment in the police force'.

The Bastar region of Chhattisgarh has also been the site of the activities of the Salwa Judum (meaning 'purification hunt'). This militia was set up with the approval of the government in 2005, at the instigation of a sometime Communist, later Congress MLA (Member of the Legislative Assembly), Mahendra Karma. This was framed by Karma—who has been charged for his involvement in a conspiracy over the theft of forest rights—as a popular and 'Gandhian' movement of tribal people against the Naxalites. In practice, there is strong evidence of the responsibility of the Salwa Judum, with Special Police Officers, for the use of considerable violence in forcing large-scale displacements of people to roadside camps: Sundar gives the figure of 46,000, Miklian figures of 60,000 according to government or 40,000 according to independent estimates. Large areas have effectively been laid waste. Many villages have been destroyed. The actions of the Salwa Judum have given rise to warlordism with some of warlords being outsiders from North India, who are supporters of Hindu fundamentalism. The Movement rapidly ceased to be under the control either of Karma or the police. Miklian notes, for instance, that in September 2007, 'Access to Dornapal Police HQ is controlled by Kuhwal (one of these warlords from North India) as the police chief of Dornapal needs to ask his permission to allow visitors or make tactical decisions'. There is a very long catalogue of human rights violations in Chhattisgarh, as Miklian reports. Even the Frontline report, more sympathetic to Salwa Judum than others records, 'Though Salwa Judum was well-intentioned, (a point that would certainly be challenged by Sundar and Miklian) it soon degenerated into yet another instrument of harassment, extortion and torture'. It is seen, nonetheless, as a model to be emulated in other states (Jharkhand and Maharashtra, according to Miklian). Chhattisgarh illustrates very starkly the spiral of violence associated with Maoism. It also illustrates the interconnections of politicians, private companies and both Maoists and anti-Maoist forces that lead to the reproduction of conflict, because so many powerful actors benefit from it.

As a way of defeating the Maoists, the Salwa Judum has not proven successful—indeed there are reports that its actions have encouraged fresh recruitment to them—but Salwa Judum 'is in many ways a complete success, operating exactly as its founders intended, as a land and power grab masquerading as local uprising'. Miklian proceeds to argue that finding a solution to the security problem that is presented in Bastar is 'problematised by the fact that every major actor (in Chhattisgarh) gains more from continued conflict than peace'. In the Dantewara area of Bastar, it is iron that generates the funding to supply all sides in the conflict. There is a publicly owned iron ore processing plant and both Essar and Tata Steel are active. Mine officials, both public and private, pay off both Salwa Judum and the Maoists. In this case, as in other parts of the 'red corridor', it appears that the existence of important natural resources is a major factor amongst the causes of enduring conflict. There is some debate amongst those who have undertaken large-n cross country analyses of the determinants of insurgency and civil wars on the significance of natural resources, with the principal protagonists being Collier and his coauthors from Oxford who think that there is a significant relationship, while Fearon and Laitin from Stanford University find that there may not be. In the 'red corridor', the presence of natural resources appears unquestionably to be a factor, though probably one that is less significant than the fact that insurgency is favoured in forested, hill areas—a point that also comes out strongly from the large-n studies.

But it is not only the extremely valuable mineral resources of the region—such as Orissa's high quality bauxite—that give the key actors material interests in the continuation of conflict. Bert Suykens has analysed what he describes as a 'relatively stable joint extraction regime' operates in the trade in tendu leaves, used in making beedi cigarettes, in the tribal areas of the Telengana region of Andhra. 'This low profile, lootable resource' provides the single most important source of income both for tribals in North Telengana (during the summer season) and the Maoists. Both the state and the Naxalites hold some degree of public authority and exercise it, in effect jointly, to control the trade and extract resources from it. The analysis shows how:

> Naxalite authority has been able to extend its influence over the wages of [tendu leaf] collectors, the appointment of khalledars [purchase agents], the earning of revenue and to a lesser extent, certain aspects of the beedi manufacturing industry. In this role of public authority, the Naxalites do not conform to their popular image as either weapon-wielding terrorists or the vanguard of social-activism. At the same time, the Indian state does not seem to be able to prevent the Naxalites from taking up this role. Although the state clearly has the overall advantage, both in manpower and money, and provides the framework for the trade in beedi, the Naxalites seem to have a comparative advantage in controlling the day-to-day working of the trade.

Alpa Shah, with regard to a region of Jharkhand, has argued that the Naxalites there became very much like the state, selling protection in return for support. They call it 'taxation' and the income from their levies on the tendu leaf trade or on the building of roads, bridges and dams, are a crucial source of income for their operations. Navlakha records that the annual budget of an Area Revolutionary People's Committee in the territory of the Jantanam Sarkar in Bastar was 'made up of Rs. 360,000 in taxes on contractors, Rs. 500,000 allotted by the Jantanam Sarkar [origins of these funds not specified] and Rs. 250,000 collected through work days or shram daan by households in the area'. He subsequently describes the revenues of the Party as follows.

> 'Most of the money was now collected in the form of royalty on tendu patta, bamboo, tamarind and other forest produce. Revenue from looting banks or confiscating wealth was far less. They did tax some of the companies and contractors who operated in what they describe as the guerilla zone. In any case their sources were indigenous and not external, which even the government was forced to concede'.

The Maoists to build an alliance between the proletariat, peasantry, petty-bourgeoisie and national bourgeoisie. They have been influenced both by caste and local politics. There are instances where one or other Naxalite group has entered an area through winning the support of members of upper castes and the rural middle classes. The pattern of support may shift over time as in Central Bihar according to Kunnath's account. Revolutionary groups there have sought to win over powerful upper castes in their quest to secure state power, losing support amongst Dalits and others in the process. The lines of class conflict may be blurred by these factors.

The coming together of the major groups to form the CPI(Maoist) in 2004 marked a turning point and the Movement is now recognised as constituting the most serious challenge to its authority that the Indian state has ever confronted. The Maoists have gained strength from the failures of the state in regard to large numbers of poor people. There have been extensive failures of omission relating to the delivery of public services and social security, and failures of commission having to do with the abuses to which people have been subjected at the hands of the police, the forest department and other officials. Close observers have found that ordinary people in areas where the Maoists are well-organised have more faith in them than they do in the state. Actual or threatened displacement of large numbers especially of tribal people to make way for mining, power generation or other projects has given rise to resistance movements with which the Maoists have often been associated, if they have not actually organised them. Rents derived from natural resources such as the minerals of Bastar and Orissa or trade such as tendu leaves in northern Telengana or from supplying protection provide the funds for carrying on administration in the areas that the Maoists now control and for supporting armed struggle. These rents may make for incentives to keep conflict going. The essential reason, however, for the strength of the Maoists in the hilly, forested tracts of eastern and central India is that this terrain, in India as elsewhere in the world, most favours guerilla insurgency. Though it has been argued that 'there are hardly any reliable empirical studies to measure the level of support or to weigh the reasons for the common people to join the movement', the ethnographic studies and some other reports cited in this review, clearly show that the Naxalites/Maoists have won support from amongst landless and poor peasants, Dalits and adivasis—and probably particularly amongst young men and women who have limited opportunities. They also show that the Maoists have had some positive impacts upon the lives and livelihoods of such people in many places. At best, they have changed rural power relations; more generally, they have enhanced the self-respect of poor people. Political leaders such as Digvijay Singh and others argue that it will only be when the state effectively addresses these problems that it will win people back. In their view, the Maoists cannot be defeated by sheer force. Gautam Navlakha, in the first of the epigraphs to this paper, based on his experiences in Bastar concurs: 'this is one rebellion which will test the resilience of the Indian state as never before. Precisely because it is a rebellion in which people are fighting to save their land, forests, water and minerals from being grabbed and they are convinced that they have an alternative vision'. The actions of state security forces and especially of those that are allowed to operate outside the law (such as Salwa Judum), often in support of private capital invested in mining and other projects in tribal areas that are likely not to benefit local people, continually provide reasons for such people to support the Maoists. The very uncertainty that is created in people's everyday lives in these conflict situations may very well prompt some people to join the Maoists as a way of trying to find 'certainty' for themselves as Shah has argued.

At the same time, even sympathetic observers like Balagopal, Banerjee and Bhatia think that the violence that is inevitably a part of the Maoists' activity—given their commitment to armed struggle, which they see as necessary and unavoidable—leads to disconnection between the Maoist leadership and followers. This is what Balagopal observed in the differences in the attitudes towards the Maoists of people from different generations in Andhra Pradesh and what Bhatia feared had happened in Central Bihar. This lends credence, of course, to the views of those like Simeon and Nigam who see in Maoism a middleclass/upper caste intelligentsia 'playing out revolutionary fantasies'. Those few scholars and activists who have undertaken studies in areas in which the Maoists are strong report the pragmatism in the attitudes of many ordinary people. The Maoists often seem regarded as being more trustworthy than the representatives of the state but this faith in them does not extend to support for their ideology or their methods. It is the tragedy of the politics of armed struggle that it is a response to the appalling structural violence that has been perpetrated historically and that continues to be perpetrated by elites, supported by the state, against landless and poor peasants, Dalits and adivasis, and yet it leads to a spiral of violence in which the same people may become trapped. As noted historian Ramachandra Guha has said:

> There is a double tragedy at work... The first tragedy is that the state has treated its adivasi [and other poor and marginalised] citizens with contempt and condescension. The second tragedy is that their presumed protectors, the Naxalites, offer no long-term solution either.

4

Changing Pattern in Naxalite Movement

It may be noted that barring a few interventions, writings and books which reached the newsstands in the immediate aftermath of Naxalbari, the whole gamut of revolutionary left movement has largely remained outside the purview of Indian Marxist intellectuals of different hues all these years. It is only when gross human rights violations are noticed in the naxalite infested (as the bourgeois press calls it) areas that one observes activities on part of the partisan intelligentsia. But by and large the concerns and the experiences, programmes, strategies and tactics, interorganisational relationships have largely remained unanalysed and undiscussed among left intellectuals. Definitely no single individual can be held responsible for this, but it need be said that maintaining silence over such a big social phenomenon does not seem to be a healthy trend.

THE PARADOXES OF THE RISING OF NAXALITE MOVEMENT

Today the revolutionary left movement loosely called the

Naxalite movement presents quite a paradoxical picture. One notices two processes, the first one signifying its progress on practical and on a limited theoretical plane and the other one signifying the problems since its inception which have maintained a continuity with the past.

On the one hand all evidence goes to show that the movement is on the rise, its influence among the poor and downtrodden is growing. Despite tremendous state repression accompanied by martyrdoms and killings, Andhra being the most strife torn state, the flow of fresh cadres to its ranks is not dwindling. It is not for nothing that today it can claim to be one of the strongest revolutionary left movements in the world, those only next to the Philippines, Peru and Nepal.

Fresh action plan on part of the government seeking Vietnamese or Israeli help in the counterinsurgency operations against the Naxalites are also an indicator that all the old grandiose plans about its suppression have come a cropper and the movement as a whole is growing.

On the other hand it is also true that the revolutionary left has been beset with problems which are refusing to go. If the problem of left adventurism visited it in the earlier period, today also it can't be said with surity that the movement has got rid of this trend. Left adventurism coupled with right opportunism present the strongest non-proletarian trend within the movement.

As things stand today the revolutionary left has been marked by the presence of more than forty odd formations and the tragic phenomenon of split within split. The failure of the movement in impacting the national politics all these years barring a small period at the time of the Naxalite uprising and its essentially marginal existence on the scene appears quite natural in such a background.

Definitely this paradoxical situation needs to be explained before talking about the future prognosis of the movement. One needs to delve deep into the strengths and the weaknesses of the movement and simultaneously one should also look into the whole dialectic of subjective forces and objective conditions logic to arrive at a clear understanding.

A comprehensive understanding of this paradoxical situation requires analysis at three different levels. The first and foremost can be said to be the problems encountered in the initial phase of the movement. The second layer of analysis would comprise of the programmatic formulations adopted by the movement and its relevance in today's conditions. The third layer of analysis should focus on the changes in the overall schema of global capital and the challenges before the socialist project in the aftermath of the reversals faced by the socialist camp.

Before delving deep into the pluses and the minuses of the movement it would be better to cast a glance at the contemporary Naxalite movement which has acquired a different look since the days of Naxalbari. Ranging from geographical shift to a new crop of leadership this new face is visible at many different levels.

The most significant change has been the plethora of formations which today claim the legacy of the Naxalite uprising. It could be said that all the attempts since the days of Naxalbari to unite the revolutionary communists under a single banner have failed. And indications are that nothing substantial will happen in the coming years.

The old leadership of the movement has given way to an altogether new leadership which had its first brush with politics in the aftermath of Naxalbari. Most of the old stalwarts of the movement are either dead or not playing any significant role.

The second noticeable change has been an areawise shift in the focus of the movement. If Bengal heralded the onset of the "Naxalbari uprising" adding names of Naxalbari, Debra-Gopiballabpur, Birbhum, Calcutta, etc. to the folklore then, today with more than two decades of rule by CPIM the revolutionary left has been relegated to the background in that state, and movements in Bihar and Andhra Pradesh, Madhya Pradesh, etc. have gained prominence.

A sea change is visible in the modus operandi of the movement. None of the formations owing allegiance to Naxalbari today considers building mass organisations to be a sign of "revisionism"; most of them at some level are engaged in what would have been considered "reformist work", in the earlier phase; many of the formations have started fighting elections supposedly to expose the system; nobody now talks of red armies marching in the would be "Yenans" of India.

Another notable feature is the changed composition of class forces standing or supporting the movement. If in the 60s revolutionary left could garner enough support based among the urban middle classes in general and the intelligentsia in particular, especially in Bengal, leading the famous exodus of the "best brains of the times" to join with the movement. Down the years the whole movement has acquired a predominantly rural or tribal character where lower castes and marginal groups in [the] social hierarchy now form the core of its support base.

A significant change is also noticeable as far as sustaining the movement in any particular area for long period is concerned. At the time of Naxalbari it was not possible to continue at the high pitch of struggle for long. The uprising in Naxalbari could continue only for around seventy two days. The "guerilla" struggle which essentially got reduced to the line of "annihilation" of class enemies in areas like Srikakulam, Debra-Gobiballapur, [and] Birbhum also could not be sustained for long.

Today the movements in Gadchiroli in Maharashtra, Bastar in Madhya Pradesh or Koraput in Orrissa etc. apart from the strong movements in Dandakaranya and central Bihar are witness to the change that has occurred at the ground level.

Of course beneath the new look one notices quite a few things which are continuing in the same vigour and same mode. First and foremost seems to be the ideological zeal of its cadres who are committed to the cause of socialism and in a majority of cases ready to do ultimate sacrifice for this goal.

Like in late 60s it is still in a position to channelise the frustration of a large section of the thinking section of the Indian people over the failure of the independence project. Its making a radical rupture in the early days with parliamentarism and economism which had crept into the left movement and till [this] date it's largely keeping itself aloof from the mire of electoral politics and focussing attention on raising people's struggles in many a militant way is also worth underlining.

Like in the days of the 'spring thunder' the focus of the movements is still on the most backward regions and terrain of India where various medieval forms of oppression still persist.

RECENT ACTIVITIES OF NAXALITE GROUPS

As an aside it would be worthwhile to throw light on some of the actual activities of Naxal groups which are rarely mentioned in the mainstream media and completely get ignored in the government pronouncements. These activities in fact, are one of the reasons for the continuing popularity of Naxal groups in parts of India. It need be noted that what follows is a random selection of news and reports purportedly to give an idea of the multifarious activities undertaken by various ML formations.

Vaartha, Eenadu and all other leading newspapers of A P reported in May 1996 the temple entry movement led by Progressive Organisation of People, an outfit affiliated to the revolutionary left movement, in a village called Gudipadu situated around 20 km away from Kurnool, Andhra Pradesh. According to the newspapers the local Reddys and other upper class people denied the entry to the people belonging to Madiga community, a caste coming under scheduled category, to a temple constructed on village common land. The movement that ensued which had participation of different organisations from all over the state ultimetely proved successful.

It may also be told that the same organisations took up similar cases of caste apartheid or discrimination in many adjoining villages.

In a report on Naxalites under the title "Love for the Outlaws", Kanhaiah Bhelari tells us that ". . . .Naxalites are the most loved lot in south Bihar not for nothing. In fact, they are the people's only insurance against demanding policemen, criminals and landlords." According to him the MCC and People's War Group have opened several schools in their areas of influence. Prominent among them are the ones in Matlaung (managed by MCC) and Baruwaiya (managed by PWG) in Palamu district.

He further adds that even some police superintendents were appreciative of the Naxalite crime control activities. District courts in the Naxal dominated areas have been witnessing a substantial drop in cases coming to them. In Palamu alone the number of cases dropped from an average of 2400 per year to 1600 in the year 1997.

Many leading newspapers from the capital reported about the uproar in the Lok Sabha in the budget session (year 2000) of the parliament over the fast unto death undertaken by Umadhar Singh, MLA from Bihar owing allegiance to CPI(ML) New Democracy to demand CBI inquiry into the irregularities committed in the closure of Ashok Paper Mill. As already reported the MLA was seeking an inquiry into the alleged siphoning away of Rs. 7 crore of central aid given for revival of a sick paper mill in Bihar.

In a seminar organised by All India People's Resistance Forum, Prof Manoranjan Mohanty, Delhi University while delivering his speech on the human rights situation reported that the ". . . police and paramilitary forces destroyed a big irrigation bund, near Mahbob Nagar, (A.P.) built by voluntary labour, since the inspiration came from the Naxalites. Police also destroyed five bus stops in Karim Nagar and Warangal district since they were built by sympathizers of the Naxalite movement. He gave several such instances of the attitude of the police towards development programmes run by the Naxals".

People's Union for Civil Liberties in an illuminating report on Baster more than a decade ago has this to say about the movement led by Naxalites there ". . . a lopsided socioeconomic development of the district caused by indirect exploitation through environmental destruction and direct exploitation through cheating and duping, has provided an ideal setting for the Naxalites to take root in the area. . . . They supported the illegal encroachments of forest land and organised some campaigns of encroachment themselves; they repeatedly brought to the fore the issue of tanks and the need to maintain them in a systematic manner for irrigation; they openly opposed the Bodhghat project; they punished corrupt officials; they made the tendu leaf contractors increase the wage rates; and they held health and education programmes among tribals".

In his celebrated travelogue India Waits, Jan Myrdal a Swedish national and author of many a book, opined favourably about the activities of the armed squads belonging to one of the groups (CP Reddy group) of the ML movement. The area covered by Jan and his wife was Warangal. According to him the armed squads are political organizers, not anarchists or bandits.

The job of the squad is to popularise the revolutionary line and to take up the people's problems. Each squad is made up of a squad leader and four members. According to him 90 percent of the squad members they met were natives of the local areas. "The armed squads teach new improved farming methods. They help people carry out irrigation projects. Just in this area (Warangal) we've seen [. . .] that thirty irrigation reservoirs have been built".

He further adds that cultural work is an important part of the squad's work which includes not only songs and dances but political education and teaching [the] three R's forms the key component of this work. About the integration of the Naxalites with the life of the common people Jan Myrdal is all praise and tells how Subba becomes Subbanna (elder brother Subba) or Nirmala becomes Nirmalakka (elder sister Nirmala) and the party secretary becomes Pedanna (the eldest).

Prakash Singh, an IPS officer who was posted some time in Naxalite infested areas to oversee the operations, in his book The Naxalite Movement in India says ". . . [s]horn of politics, it (the Naxalite movement) represents the struggle of the exploited peasant, deprived tribal and the urban proletariat for a place in the sun, for social and economic survival." While looking at the genesis of the ups and downs of the movement he adds, "Naxalism arose from certain basic factors-social injustice, economic inequality and the failure of the system to redress the grievances of a large sections of people who suffered and continue to suffer as a result therefrom".

While acknowledging that the Naxalite movement could attract some of the finest brains and the cream of India's youth in certain areas, who left their homes and colleges to chase the dream of a new world, a new social order, he concludes that "The factors which gave rise to Naxalism in the country are, in any case, [are] very much present today also and in an acute and aggravated form."

As already mentioned since late 60s when the Naxalite uprising occurred much water has flown down the Tista or for that matter the Ganges. Gone are the days when the pioneers of the movement propagated that "the battle of annihilation of class enemies is both the higher form of class struggle and the starting point of guerilla war" or when mass organisations and mass movements were supposed to increase the tendency towards open and economistic movement or when dependence upon petty bourgeois intellectuals along with disregard for mass forms led to emphasis on individual terrorism based on conspiratorial methods. "The method of forming a guerilla unit has to be wholly conspiratorial. . . This conspiracy should be between intellectuals and on a person to person basis. The petty bourgeois intellectual comrade should take initiative in this respect as far as possible. He should approach the poor peasant who in his opinion has the most revolutionary potentiality and whisper in his ears: Don't you think it a good idea to finish off such a jotedar?" [Or the] declaration of "China's Chairman" to be "our Chairman" or declaring [the] 70s to be decade of emancipation was witnessed during this period only.

THE REVOLUTIONARY MASS LINE

Definitely the new face of the movement would not have been possible had the leadership of the movement continued its journey on these and similar "left adventurist deviations" and had not abandoned many of its wrong formulations. Within the All India Coordination Committee of Communist Revolutionaries which was formed in the aftermath of the Naxalite Uprising to unite the "revolutionaries of CPM" also one witnessed the struggle against this adventurist deviations.

In fact it can be said that the first major struggle within the incipient revolutionary left movement around the question of revolutionary mass line was led by T Nagi Reddy, D V Rao, veterans of the Communist movement from A P. Today the whole spectrum of the revolutionary left looks more akin to be working on the tactical line of the A P Revolutionary Communist Committee led by T Nagi Reddy and D V Rao. It may sound one of the ironies of history that the APRCC was disaffiliated from the All India Coordination Committee of Communist Revolutionaries over basic differences which essentially boiled down to loyalty to CPC, differences regarding people's armed struggle and differences regarding boycotting elections.

Most of the formations have been compelled by circumstances to review past mistakes and have to draw necessary lessons therefrom. Of course it can't be said that an all round critique of the left adventurist positions including its genesis and growth and its impact on the organisational line has been done by the movement. For that the very formation of the CPI(ML) which took place under the shadow of this left adventurist position only and was declared soon after the disaffiliation of APRCC needs to be scrutinized again.

Overall the situation is such that the forty plus formations in which the movement has split have gotten over the blatant manifestations of the wrong line which raised its head in the initial period. But at a deeper level it appears that many of the remnants of the older understanding are still continuing. The correct approach towards revolutionary mass line is yet to evolve and to be articulated.

ATTITUDES TOWARD ELECTIONS

One also notices diametrically opposite positions on tactical matters. For example, a significant section of the ML formations still are carriers of the boycott elections line. The inconsistency of the "boycottists" is also visible when they are found to be tactically supporting this or that bourgeois formation under the general slogan of election boycott.

Whereas quite a few formations have rectified their approach towards elections but now another danger is visible when a major formation within this block seems to be drifting towards CPI-CPM to form what it calls left confederation.

THE LEFT ADVENTURISM OF THE EARLY MOVEMENT

What could be said to be the genesis of the left adventurism witnessed in the initial phase of the movement? One reason could be [that] the drift to left adventurism was a logical culmination of the one and a half decade history of parliamentarism and economism rampant in the movement after the "abject surrender of Telangana people's armed struggle" when the pendulum swung to an opposite direction.

A correct approach to this initial phase of the movement can be set if we revisit the question of the evaluation of Charu Mazumdar's role. While the historic role played by the ideological leadership of Charu Mazumdar in this radical rupture from the "neo-revisionist" CPM needs to be highlighted, it cannot be denied that his leadership held the principal responsibility for fomenting a left adventurist line.

It will be a separate study in itself to know how adventurism essentially negates democracy and promotes centralism and how it affects proper organisational functioning. In the Indian case it precipitated the phenomenon of splits which continues till [the present] date.

The AICCR in its very first declaration had stated that one of its main tasks would be "to undertake preparations of a revolutionary programme and tactical line based on concrete analysis of Indian conditions in the light of Mao Tse Tung's thought". History is witness to the fact that this task could not be accomplished because of the dominance of left adventurist line which saw the formation of the CPI(ML) just after the disaffiliation of the APRCC led by T Nagi Reddy and D V Rao and scuttling the first great debate in the ML movement around revolutionary mass line.

THE FORMULATIONS OF INDIA AS "SEMI-FEUDAL" AND "SEMI-COLONIAL"

The 1970 programme accepted by the [newly] formed CPI(ML) stated that "India is semi-feudal and semi-colonial country, the Indian state is the state of the big landlords and comprador bureaucrat capitalists and its government is a lackey of U.S imperialism and Soviet social imperialism". It further said that "the Indian revolution at this stage is the democratic revolution of the new type-the People's Democratic Revolution-the main content of which is the agrarian revolution". According to this understanding, by building [a] strong worker-peasant alliance and following Mao's theory of protracted people's war revolutionary communists will be able to give crushing blows to the powerful enemies and usher into a new democratic revolution.

A majority of the formations belonging to the revolutionary left stream still broadly accept this programme. But it is interesting to note that while adhering to this programme their interpretation and understanding of this line does not converge. While for some in the binary combination of feudalism and imperialism, feudalism is acting as the main contradiction, a small section in this spectrum also talks of the alliance of feudalism-imperialism to be the basic contradiction. With passage of time the earlier assertions regarding "China's Path to be Our Path" or the blind application of the Chinese experience [to the] Indian situation have been de-emphasized. The differences of the Indian situation vis-a-vis [the] Chinese situation have slowly got prominence. There is growing recognition of the development of capitalism in various spheres of society and its impacting the social relations.

Questions are also being asked about the whole concept of "semi feudal" relations which was based on the premise that feudalism acted as a social prop of imperialism as was evident during the times of Chinese revolution. The actual transformation of the Indian agriculture undertaken with the abolition of intermediaries or with the emergence of the new class of kulaks and rural proletariat has prompted its comparison with that of the Junker transformation of agriculture in the 19th century Prussia. As is known, [the] Junker path or the Prussian path of agrarian transformation focussed on the non-revolutionary manner in which agriculture in the feudal mode could be put on the capitalist path. Lenin's study on the The Development of Capitalism in Russia has helped initiate debate within the movement to discern the underlying development of productive forces and the changes in production relations in the Indian context. The criteria set forth by Lenin regarding [the] development of capitalism in agriculture namely, extraction of surplus through employment of wage labour, general commoditization and widespread existence of market relations and transformation of surplus into capital for facilitating extended reproduction of capitalism have facilitated this discussion.

Later studies have further helped to know the multifarious ways in which capital enters agriculture. Practical experience of different movements in rural areas also prompted discussion on the characterisation of Indian agriculture. Semi-feudal production relations connote that [the] four class alliance involving rich peasants, middle peasants and poor as well as landless peasants or agricultural workers would come up against "feudal lords". Barring some pockets in far off areas one noticed that it is failing to come up, and by and large [a] three class alliance comprising middle, poor peasants and agricultural workers [is] emerging where the middle peasant acts as a vacillating ally of the revolutionary forces.

The concept of "semi-colonial" has also come under fresh scrutiny. Naxalbari happened when the whole world appeared to be taking a new turn when the Indian ruling classes were caught up in the first major crisis in post-colonial India, or when many a capital of the advanced capitalist countries were ringing with anti-capitalist slogans accompanied by large scale mass movements. It was a time when France witnessed [the] student worker uprising in May '68 or a strong antiwar movement erupted in US or when the growing anti-colonial struggles in many African and Asian countries were sort of providing a living proof that they have become storm centres of revolution, or when tiny Vietnam was delivering death blows to U S Imperialism.

Today with the completion of the task of liberation of colonies leading to emergence of independent nation states and with the unfolding of the phenomenon of globalisation of capital it is becoming clear that the old characterisation should be given a fresh thought. In the Indian context the way in which the Indian bourgeoisie has gathered strength and enlarged its base without unleashing a revolutionary onslaught on feudalism and without making a break with imperialism is being noted by everyone.

It is true that its success in establishing its leadership over the anti-colonial struggle and its taking advantage of the major developments on the international arena has helped it achieve such a position. The task of decolonisation undertaken by the Indian bourgeoisie to remove colonial distortions from the economy but at the same time making compromises with imperialism and preparing the ground for entering into a partnership with the imperialist capital for the exploitation of Indian people further point to the inadequacy of the older formulation depicting its relationship with imperialism.

The imposition of emergency by the Indira regime which was frightened by the unfolding crisis and growing people's movement way back in 1975 precipitated [a] questioning process on the "semi-colonial" mode in the revolutionary left movement. [The question] was raised [about] how a "comprador bourgeoisie" which is nothing but "stooge of imperialism" could grant "limited democratic rights" to its people.

THE 1970 PROGRAMME NEEDS TO BE UPDATED

It is becoming more and more clear that the 1970 programme, which was based on the then existing understanding of [the] interrelationship between feudalism and imperialism and was written in the shadow of the new strides taken by the Chinese revolution, needs to be either updated or dealt afresh. The salient features of the Indian situation also need to be detailed out. It should comprise not only the specificities of the Indian state and society as they have evolved down the years but also incorporate the strength as well as limitations of the revolutionary left's intervention in terms of theory as well as practice and [the] trajectory of its relationship with other people's movements [and] struggles.

The texture of times can also be demonstrated by half a century of experiment in bourgeois democracy which has helped strengthen various misconceptions and illusions about this mode of governance. It would not be an exaggeration to say that the situation encountered by the revolutionary left in India today is unique of its kind [and] without any precedence. The Great revolutions of the 20th century mainly occurred confronting a state which was more backward, more barbaric and denied even a semblance of democratic rights to its citizenry.

The revolutionary left in India has to confront a state which has also learned from the negative experiences of these revolutions for itself and has been able to spread bourgeois democracy by multifarious ways which includes regular election to various representive bodies or granting limited democratic rights to the citizens.

It is also clear that [the] state is very selective in the application of its repressive laws and machinery. Whereas it has for all practical purposes imposed martial law like situations in North East or Kashmir or the various strongholds of the revolutionary left where the police and paramilitary forces have been given tremendous powers in one or the other variant of Armed Forces Special Powers Act, in the rest of India it has still been able to largely maintain democratic pretensions with the spread out network of judiciary, executive and legislature at various levels of society.

The uneven development of India with the concomitant existence of various castes, communities and nationalities has compounded the task further in one way or the other. As already mentioned the end of the 20th century has been witness to new types of movements ranging from the dalit, women, to issues of sustainable development. And it already been mentioned that the revolutionary left has largely remained on the periphery of these movements. Though at practical level of grassroot politics it has shown lot of innovativeness and creativity by raising the question of izzat and its initial success in central Bihar can be attributed to its realising the importance of this issue but as far as theoretical backup is concerned it seems to be still embroiled in the traditional "class reductionist" framework.

The issue of gender oppression and an end to patriarchy has also to be dealt with in a more creative manner. Looking at the spread of the movement it has already been discussed that it is more strong in those areas where mediaeval forms of oppression still exist or violation of minimum democratic norms is the order of the day. The other part of the story is that it has yet to make a headway in those normal areas where a semblance of democratic apparatus still operates or where the issues of izzat do not exits at mass level or for that matter community or tribal bondage hardly exist. Its more or less absence from the urban India barring a few pockets in some stray cities or its below marginal presence in the organised working class is definitely a cause of concern.

It is also true that it has to get ready to answer many inconvenient questions which it has till now brushed aside as part of bourgeois propaganda. The human rights movements in this country which has all along protested encounter killings and violation of democratic rights, has recently raised some questions about the implementation of democratic rights within the movement. Definitely this is an altogether changed terrain than the one when the first salvos of Naxalbari reverberated throughout India.

The revolutionary left has to clearly understand that these are new times which demand a lot of imaginary and creativity and persistence from the torchbearers of [the] genuine left. The task of building an all India revolutionary communist party needs to be taken up with new vigour. First and foremost fresh attempts need to be done to reverse the phenomenon of splits within splits and unify the various apparently heterogeneous formations under a single umbrella.

Definitely [there must] ensue a period of intense debates, discussions and polemical exchanges within the formations to reach a unified understanding of ideological, political and organisational positions. If the movement does not show enough perseverance to undertake these tasks there is a danger that the movement will not be able to stop its slide into the cesspool of militant economism or right opportunism.

Revolutions happen not only because the objective conditions are ripe or the subjective forces are well organised, the necessary condition for any such situation is that the leading elements should be in a position to provide blueprint of revolution at least at a theoretical level. It has two aspects: Firstly, the leading elements should be able to provide a correct appraisal of the then existing national-international situation and secondly, they should be in a position to give a scientific and balanced critique about the socialist project as it unfolded and [the] future prognosis of the same.

The revolutionary left as it exists and operates today, will have to take up this with right earnestness if it really wants to leave its imprint on the 21st century. First and foremost it will have to get to know the challenges presented by the times.

Apart from the earthshaking events like the colonial countries becoming storm centres of revolution, Naxalbari happened when under the leadership of Mao Tse Tung the Great Proletarian Cultural Revolution had unleashed a historic struggle to save the nascent socialist state from taking a capitalist road. As is history the Great Proletarian Cultural Revolution was accompanied by formation of revolutionary communist parties the world over which came out of the parent "pro-soviet parties". And in many places these parties had launched armed struggle to follow the Chinese path against their ruling classes who according to them were lackeys of imperialism and epitome of feudal reaction.

Today all that is over. Neither the socialist bloc is to be seen and the then centre of world proletarian revolution China itself has undertaken great strides on the capitalist road. As things stand today the national and international situation is less conducive and more adversarial for any movement which claims to fight for social justice and progress.

The revolutionary left needs to understand the changed terrain and its different contours as it is obtained in the beginning of the 21st century to make a correct appraisal of the situation. Essentially it needs to give a fresh look at the three large questions before itself. First, how has the world capitalist system changed over the course of this century and what is the modus operandi of imperialism today? What has been the extensive and intensive changes in the way capitalism operates? Second, how to review and what lessons to draw from the history of socialism as it existed during the twentieth century? And third, what future courses are open to the societies of the third world countries which have made varying degrees of transition to capitalism? What are the prospects of revolution in these countries and what is likely to be the nature and the course of these revolutions?

Definitely these are not simple questions and in the present conditions as they are obtained in the revolutionary movement they are largely open questions. Nobody can claim today to have adequate answers to all or any of them. It would be one of the key tasks of the international communist movement to work out these answers.

SUMMING UP

It is pertinent to ask what did the Naxalites achieve in their three plus decade old rebellion. And a part of the answer could be provided by quoting Samar Sen, the famous Bengali poet and founder editor of Frontier in his editorial note to "Naxalbari and After: A Frontier Anthology": "[but] What did Naxalbari achieve in practical terms? The cynic might ask. And it is a difficult question to answer. Admittedly, the Naxalbari raised more problems than they solved. But the very problems they raised and tried to solve in a hurry had never been raised with such a force of sincerity before or after Telengana. That is their achievement."

Definitely it has not been an easy task for the Naxalites to break new grounds in the left movement to retrieve the revolutionary essence of Marxism. Of course its pioneers would not have thought that it would prove to be such a tortuous process that [since] the decade of the 70s which was declared to be a decade of liberation, the beginning of the 21st century would also find them quite far away from their cherished goal of ushering into a People's India.

The '90s symbolized the paradoxical situation of the movement in a poignant manner. On the one hand it witnessed escalation of violence on part of the state to contain what it calls "ideology clad left wing extremism" leading to sharp increase in the number of encounter killings or its bold pronouncements about forming a joint command for Naxalite affected areas.

On the other hand the phenomenon of internecine killing among different revolutionary groups raised its head with a vengeance in this decade only. While one could trace the genesis of these types of violent internecine disputes in the 80s, it could only make its presence felt [when] the 90s situation came to such a pass that the private armies of the landlords like Ranveer Sena could raise their head in Bihar benefiting from the internecine armed disputes.

Of course on the positive side one was witness to [a] new realisation, [a] new appreciation of the changed terrain and the texture of times in which the revolutionary left has to negotiate its path and supposedly make break through in the 21st century. The positive reaction and the debate generated in the whole spectrum of the revolutionary left over a study on Globalisation of Capital brought out by CLI(ML) can be called a sign of the times to come.

The importance of international linkages with a vision to form a new international is also becoming more and more clear. There have been quite a few international seminars in which various streams of the revolutionary left participated. Groups like CPI(ML) JanShakti and People's War also took [the] initiative in organising international seminars in their home country. The unity of CPI(ML) People's War Group and CPI(ML) Party Unity under a single banner has also helped embolden the mood among the genuine sympathisers of the movement.

Will [the] Naxalite left be able to get out of this anomalous situation in which it finds itself today? Will it prove to be [the] real inheritors of the Bolsheviks who ushered us into the first socialist revolution or it will get sucked into the Charkavuva much like the mythological Abhimanyu from Mahabharata who it is said did not know the correct way to get out of the battle? Whether the new century would help the whole spectrum of revolutionary left turn a new leaf in the history of communist movement in the 21st century. The situation is pregnant with tremendous new possibilities. It remains to be seen whether the Naxalite left which carved out a place for itself in postcolonial India in the 20th Century will be able to repeat its feat in the contemporary India.

5

Naxalite Movement in Bihar

People living free from poverty and despair and with full security and dignity are still the world's preferred dream. The human security approach, popularized by institutions such as the UNDP and the Human Security Network, and by scholars such as Mahbub ul Haq and Amartya Sen, claims to detail the possibility of realizing this dream in concrete terms. Often referred to as 'people-centred security' or 'security with a human face', the human security approach is defined in terms of two supposedly mutually-inclusive conceptual phrases: 'freedom from fear'; and 'freedom from want'. Safety is the hallmark of 'freedom from fear', while well-being is the goal of 'freedom from want'. On the basis of data from rural Bihar one can argues that 'freedom from fear' and 'freedom from want' are not necessarily connected. On the one hand, the Naxalites and their various offshoots, and on the other the formation of private caste-based militias clearly reflect the contradictions between 'freedom from fear' and 'freedom from want' in central Bihar. The Naxalites struggle using violent means for the all round well-being of the larger but weaker section of society. The private caste-based militias try to protect their caste fellows, particularly the richer and more powerful ones, from the brutal onslaught of the Naxalites by violently attack the Naxalites and their followers.

Bihar is traditionally divided into three regions: North Bihar; South Bihar (today's Jharkhand); and Central Bihar. Central Bihar comprises 14 districts viz. Patna, Gaya, Nalanda, Jahanabad, Aurangabad, Nawada, Rohtas, Bhabhua, Bhojpur, Buxar, Munger, Jamui, Shaikhpura and Lakhisarai. It was in the central region that the Naxalites first emerged and then consolidated Naxalism. It was also where the private caste-based militias began. The ensuing violence resulted in Central Bihar being characterized as the 'flaming fields'.

The agrarian structure in most parts of Central Bihar just before the abolition of the zamindari system was dominated by the landlords from two traditionally-militant upper castes—the Bhumihars and the Rajputs. Dalits or Scheduled Castes and poor Backward Castes comprised the agricultural labourers. With the ending of the zamindari system, most of the peasants were given ownership rights over the land. This led to the emergence of a middle and rich peasantry from the Backward Castes. The increasing assertiveness of Backward Caste tenants after the zamindari abolition led to a considerable decline in begar (unpaid labour) in this region. The emergence of the Backward Caste peasantry as a powerful force, and a militant mass mobilization of the poor, led many of the higher-caste landholders to quit the rural areas and move to the towns. In most cases, middle and rich Backward Caste peasants bought their land. The mass mobilization of the rich peasantry from both upper- and middle-ranking castes, together with the growing assertiveness of poor peasants, sharecroppers and farm labourers from the lower or Scheduled Castes, has evolved into a state of confrontation. The latter groups are fighting for structural change in the existing social order, whereas the landowning castes are trying to maintain the status-quo and their traditional lifestyle.

These opposing currents resulted in the emergence of Naxalism and the formation of private caste-based militias.

NAXALISM IN CENTRAL BIHAR

Naxalism was brought to the villages of Bihar in 1967; i.e., in the same year that the Naxalbari peasant revolt took place. Over the last forty years, Naxalism has engulfed almost all districts in Bihar including today's state of Jharkhand. Bella Bhatia divides the history of Naxalism in Bihar into two phases:

> Prior to the imposition of the Emergency in 1975, the movement had been able to spread in parts of two or three districts, but during the Emergency it faced heavy state persecution and had to lie low. However, by the late 1970s, it had been able to reorganise itself and was once again on an upswing. The phase after 1977, therefore, saw the revival of the movement, significant reformulations of its political line, and the emergence of new Naxalite groups.

During the formative phase from 1967 to 1977, Bihar witnessed a number of localized Naxalite struggles which were largely sporadic and were not part of a sustained and planned movement. However, the Naxalite movement that started from Ekwari Village in Bhojpur District under the leadership of Jagdish Mahato, a local teacher who had forged links with the Naxalite leaders from West Bengal, developed into a longdrawn- out organised struggle against exploitative landlords. By 1973, the Bhojpur District had become the main centre of Naxalite struggle in Bihar. By 1975, the movement had spread into four other districts of central Bihar—Gaya, Nalanda, Rohtas and Aurangabad. The intensity and magnitude of the movement's struggle took many people by surprise, but soon the whole of Central Bihar became known as the 'Flaming Fields of Bihar'.

The Naxalite movement in Bihar, as in other Indian states, is heavily factionalised. There are approximately 17 Naxalite groups operating in different parts of Bihar. The Communist Party of India (Marxist-Leninist) Liberation or CPI (ML) Liberation, the Party Unity and the Maoist Communist Centre or MCC are the most important. These three factions broadly represent the three main trends within the movement: the MCC is considered to be extreme Left; the CPI (ML) Liberation is drifting towards the 'parliamentary path'; and the Party Unity is somewhere in between.

NAXALISM AND 'FREEDOM FROM WANT'

The Naxalite Movement has been able to make significant propaganda gains regarding the idea of 'freedom from want' for the poor or weaker sections of society in Central Bihar by actively pursuing the issues concerning their basic needs and expectations. It has mainly taken up economic issues regarding (1) land rights including tenancy relations, (2) minimum wages, (3) common property resources, and (4) housing, social issues pertaining to dignity or honour and protection from organized crime, and political issues concerning citizenship including voting rights.

In Naxalite-influenced areas, one occasionally comes across a red flag determinedly planted in the middle of a field. This means that the land is contested and that the Naxalites have staked a claim to it. Usually, the landowner contests the claim, and a drawn-out battle begins. If the issue cannot be resolved through peaceful means, it often results in violent clashes. If the Naxalites win, the land is subsequently distributed to the poor for agriculture or housing. Referring to the monthly publications of various Naxalite organizations, B.N. Prasad reports that in 1992/93 the Naxalites seized 1000 acres of land in Patna District, 616 acres in Palamau, 4500 acres in Gaya and 1000 acres in Nawada and distributed it to the poor. Similar details were also published in the *Hindustan Times* (Patna, 2 August 1993).

The movement has also attempted to change tenancy relations by demanding better sharecropping terms. In some areas, the movement has successfully enforced batai (equal shares in both inputs and outputs for landowner and bataidar or tenant). In other areas it has succeeded in obtaining batai with a panja to the tenant. (Panja is the share of harvested crops given to those tenants who have harvested the crops themselves. It varies from place to place from one out of ten bundles of crops to one out of twenty.) And the movement has heavily resisted landowners' attempts to make tenants pay half of the land tax.

The struggle for just wages is another important issue taken up with considerable success by the Naxalites in Central Bihar. Prior to the coming of the Naxalite Movement, village labourers were paid not more than 2 kg of coarse rice with a simple lunch and sometimes breakfast (see Bhatia 2005: 1542), which was much less than the official minimum wage. Since the movement's intervention, the wage rate has greatly improved in many villages, and labourers receive the officially-determined wage if not more.

According to A. N. Sharma, real wage increases of 55.2 % for men and 74.3 % for women took place between 1970 and 1989 (Sharma 1997: 16). There has also been an increase in the wages paid to harvesters. Before the coming of the Naxalite Movement, as Bela Bhatia notes, 'the harvesters used to receive one bojha (headload) for every 21 bojhas of harvested crop; this has risen to 1 bojha for every 10 bojhas' (see Bhatia 2005: 1542-43). The movement's activism has also improved work conditions and fixed a reasonable number of work hours.

The Naxalite Movement has brought unity to the labourers of the area, and has made it impossible for a landlord to hire labourers if he does not satisfy their work conditions. Sometimes this unity develops into an economic blockade against a particular landlord, including the refusal of labour services. However the volatility of the situation can often lead to violence. Thus violence between workers and landlords had escalated.

The Naxalite Movement has also fought for the rights of the poor over common property resources in the villages. This has enabled the village poor to construct their houses on public or surplus land. In so doing, the movement has asserted the identity of the poor as equal members of a village.

The Naxalite Movement in Central Bihar has been fairly successfull in restoring dignity and honour to the poor and marginalized by fighting against exploitative social relations. Even though the poor continue to face many deprivations, they are now more autonomous and assertive and claim equal social space and rights in the villages.

Arbitrary beatings and instances of rape of lower-caste women have decreased dramatically. Labourers freely sell their labour to whomever they want. Dalit children go to school if their parents are willing. All this has happened because the landlords are no longer in a position to exercise their traditional power. Reports published by the People's Union for Democratic

Rights substantiate this observation. They also claim that a number of landlords have been forced by Naxalite organizations to end their feudal domination through public humiliation and punishment in the movement's Jana Adalats (People's Courts) (PUDR Report 1992).

Another important social right is the protection of the poor from violence and harassment perpetrated by organised criminal gangs generally led by the landlords of different castes. In 1978, when Party Unity first tried to build its base in Jehanabad District, it began by tackling the dominance of organized criminal gangs in the area. The Naxalite groups have been effective in targeting the most notorious gang leaders, and have considerably reduced the strength of these groups.

The poor and oppressed of Naxalite-influenced villages in Bihar are now a visible and powerful political force. They now think of themselves as citizens with the same political rights as the landlord class, and assert this equality in practice. An essential political right denied to the poor by the henchmen of the powerful castes/classes in Central Bihar was the right to vote. In areas influenced by the Naxalite Movement the poor have started exercising their right to vote (Bharti 1990). The participation in the elections of the Indian People's Front (IPF), a political institution of the CPI (ML) Liberation, has further facilitated this change. The IPF's use of the slogan 'Vote Itself' resulted in the election of an IPF candidate to the federal parliament in 1989. In the 1990 Bihar State Assembly elections, the IPF won seven seats, came second in fourteen constituencies, and third in twenty (Bharti 1990: 981). Though the participation of the IPF or CPI (ML) Liberation in the elections has not resulted in their winning many seats, it has deeply affected the nature of electoral politics.

NAXALISM, CASTE-BASED MILITIAS AND 'FREEDOM FROM FEAR'

Naxalism has undoubtedly brought about some significant changes in the highly-unequal social formation of central rural Bihar which are decisive for human development. However, it has at the same time violated all the basic principles of human rights by forcibly displacing people, making them objects of armed conflict, endangering their physical safety and security, making their living conditions worse, recruiting children for armed conflict, targeting schools and other public facilities, practising vigilante justice, destroying the means of survival of the civilian population, endlessly prolonging the conflict, and so on. It has thereby created a frighteningly hostile situation in the villages.

In so doing, Naxalism has generated tremendous problems for the realization of the idea of 'freedom from fear'—the other conceptual component of human security. Naxalism believes in Mao's dictum that political power only comes through the barrel of a gun. Therefore, the Naxalite movement remains arms-based and violent. It kills many of its enemies in extremely violent ways such as through repeatedly stabbing then slitting the victims' throats in front of other hostages. The hostages are denied food and water. The Naxalites use explosives indiscriminately including landmines to target both the security forces and civilians. They run a parallel justice system via their Jana Adalats in their strongholds which they call the 'Liberated Zones'. These deliver 'kangaroo court' justice; their enemies or so-called 'criminals' are beaten to death in full public view after the Jana Adalat pronounces the death sentence.

For more than a decade Bihar including Jharkhand has witnessed hundreds of killings every year by the Naxalites. According to the Annual Reports published by the government's Ministry of Home Affairs, the Naxalites killed 311 people in 2001, 274 in 2002, 244 in 2003, 340 in 2004, 169 in 2006 and 44 up until March 2007. In Central Bihar they carried out a number of massacres: 11 people in Darmia Village in Aurangabad District on October 7, 1986; 54 in Dalelchak-Baghaura Village in Aurangabad District on May 29, 1987; 37 in Bara Village in Gaya District on February 12, 1992; and 34 in Senari Village in Jehanabad District on March 18, 1999. One of the biggest attacks by the Naxalites in Central Bihar occurred in November 2005 when thousands of Naxalites blew up the Jehanabad police station and stormed the jail, freeing more than 300 prisoners including many fellow cadres. Over a dozen people were killed in the attack itself including three police officers. Afterwards the Naxalites segregated those who are not attached or sympathetic to them and executed them. Most of the victims were members of landowning families belonging to the dominant castes in Jehanabad District. But the Naxalites have not resrticted themselves to killing their enemies. Violent incidents leading to hundreds of death have been attributed to internecine clashes between activists of Naxalite organizations such as the MCC, Party Unity, CPI (ML) Liberation and People's War Group as each battled to establish dominance in a particular area.

State institutions have been unable to control the Naxalites. As a consequence, the dominant peasants took up their own battle cry: the peasants' lives and property are in danger and the government has failed to protect them; so the peasants themselves must protect their lives and property. At the same time, the landlords openly used the ideology of caste to counter the Naxalite Movement and the rising aspirations and assertiveness of the poor peasants and agricultural labourers. They branded the Naxalites and their supporters as merely a section of the Scheduled Castes or lower castes, and declared the Naxalite Movement to be nothing but a lower-caste movement against the interests of other castes. Accordingly, polarization along caste lines deepened while the mobilization of their caste fellows by the landlords resulted in the formation of private caste-based militias. Various caste-based militias, namely the Kuer Sena, Kunwar Sena, Bhoomi Sena, Lorik Sena, Brahmarshi Sena, Kisan Sangh, Sunlight Sena, Savarna Liberation Front, Kisan Sangha, Kisan Morcha, Ganga Sena and Ranvir Sena, were used by landlords of respective castes to fight the Naxalites and terrorize and kill low-caste villagers who they believed had provided support to the Naxalites.

The aggression perpetrated by these militias against the Naxalites and their supporters, including dalits and other weaker groups, and the latters' retaliation, has led to the routinization of violence. Hundreds of people have been killed in militia attacks. These frequently take place at night and in many cases the victims, including pregnant women and children, are killed while asleep. As well, the rape of women is a common tactic employed by the militias to spread terror among the lower castes. Although many of these militias could not sustain their existence for long and eventually petered out because of their limited cadre strength and areas of operation, the powerful Ranvir Sena, founded by the upper-caste Bhumihars in Belaur Village in Bhojpur District, is still operating. It is the most dreaded and ruthless militia group in Central Bihar. Since its inception, it has been implicated in looting, killings and rapes. It usually openly claims responsibility for its activities and even brashly announces beforehand the targeted villages.

On March 23, 1997, 10 landless labourers were killed in Haibaspur Village in Patna District, Bihar, apparently for aligning themselves with Party Unity. Before leaving the village, the Ranvir Sena inscribed its organization's name in blood on the edge of a dry well. On April 10, 1997, Ranvir Sena members gunned down eight residents of Ekwari Village in Bhojpur District. Seven of the eight killed belonged to the lower-caste Lohars, Chamars, Dhobis and Kahars. It was reported that it was the Police Force which forced open the victims' houses and then stood by and watched as the inhabitants were massacred. On December 1, 1997, Ranvir Sena activists raided fourteen dalit homes in the village of Laxmanpur-Bathe, killing at least sixty-one people and seriously injuring around twenty. As most of the men fled the village when the attack began, women and children were the main victims. At least five girls around fifteen years of age were raped and mutilated before being shot in the chest. Most of the victims allegedly belonged to the families of Party Unity supporters. The Ranvir Sena also killed around eight members of the Mallah community (a lower caste) who had had the misfortune to ferry them across the Sone River after the attack. At least twenty-two dalits including women and children died in the village of Shankarbigha in Jehanabad District on January 25, 1999. This massacre was the fifth of its kind since July 1996 in which the Ranvir Sena killed dalit and lower-caste people for their suspected allegiance to Naxalite organizations. On February 10, 1999, a little over two weeks after the Shankarbigha massacre, the Ranvir Sena killed twelve and injured seven lower-caste people by attacking neighbouring Narayanpur Village. Militia members descended on the village during the night and forced their way into homes, shooting at will. On April 21, 1999, they killed twelve persons at Sendani Village in Gaya District, and on June 16, 2000, they butchered thirtyfour inhabitants of Miapur Village in Aurangabad District (for a detailed account of the massacres, see Kumar 2008).

SUMMING UP

We can conclude by noting that even though the violent struggle led by the Naxalite Movement has a revolutionary value and to an extent has contributed to the realization of the principle of 'freedom from want', Naxalism and the concomitant terror unleashed by the private caste-based militias have created a war-like situation in Central Bihar. For many years now people of different castes and classes have been living in constant fear; they are exposed on a daily basis to the worst forms of violence which has resulted in the loss of numerous lives. Such facts problematize our understanding of the concept of human security as 'people-centred security' or 'security with a human face', by looking at the contradictions between 'freedom from fear' and 'freedom from want'. We can say, at the last, that human security principles appear to be mutually exclusive in a situation which is characterized by different forms of inequality and exploitation and which occurs in an area with a low level of development.

6

Naxalite Movement in Kerala

INTRODUCTION

The naxal challenge faced by different states in the country has heightened the interest in the study of naxalites and their ideology in recent years. Though a bulk of literature has been written on the history of naxalite movement, almost all of this focuses on the history of naxalite movement that happened in Bengal and Andhra Pradesh. But, most historians writing on this area has overlooked the fact that impact of Naxalbari revolt and Srikakulam revolt were far-reaching and in several parts of the country there were attempts to start a naxalite movement on similar lines. As the figures compiled by the Union Home Ministry indicates, from September 1967 till the middle of 1969, there has been a marked increase in the incidents of occupation of land, demonstrations demanding land for the landless, agitations for increase in wages of agricultural labourers etc. in different parts of the country. One can draw very important lessons from the study of history of rise [and fall] of naxalism in these areas.

State of Affairs: 1967-68

The naxalite movement in Kerala was inspired from the events that happened in Naxalbari village of West Bengal in 1967. In May 1967, there was an armed uprising of the peasants of Naxalbari under the leadership of Charu Majumdar and Kanu Sanyal. They were the Communist revolutionaries of the CPI(M), who was a party in the ruling United Front Government in West Bengal. They attacked police stations and landlords and had the region under their control where no outsider could enter without their permission. But by July 1967, the police was able to suppress the uprising and were able to arrest almost all major rebel leaders. Thus the uprising fizzled out without achieving anything significant.

But the Naxalbari incident had a far-reaching impact on the entire agrarian scene throughout India. The uprising, which was widely publicised, inspired the rural poor in other parts of the country to launch military struggles.

In 1968 the first of such incidents inspired from Naxalbari uprising occurred in Pulpally in Wynad and Thalassery in Kannur district of Kerala, followed by revolt in Kuttiyadi (1969) and later in Thirunelly (1970).

The naxalite attacks in Kerala were concentrated in the northern districts of Wynad and Kannur and Calicut. So it is imperative to understand the rural situation which was existing in this region which made it conducive for a revolution. The 'petty bourgeoisie' intellectuals played the vital parts in mobilising the peasants and adivasis spreading the message of Naxalbari among them. They in turn were guided by the Maoist ideology and got direct encouragement from China. Finally, we need to understand the political events that happened during this period that gave the impetus for the 'petty bourgeoisie' to rise in revolt for the cause of farmers and adivasis.

The Rural Scene

As mentioned earlier, the first attack modelled on the Naxalbari incident occurred in the Wynad region. This is because the revolutionaries thought that this region had the most conducive environment for the fostering of revolutionist ideas. The Wynad region had a major portion of the adivasi population. The Wynad valley was remarkable for its vast stretches of paddy field. Scarcity of agricultural labourers to work on the fields as serfs during the 18th century prompted the non-tribal landlords to import large numbers of adivasis (the Paniya and Adiya) from the neighboring forests that now belong to Karnataka and Tamilnadu. In Malabar the cultivating tribals were dispossessed by the influx of immigrants. Poor wages from labour on land and lack of extra avenues of employment outside agriculture drove the landless workers to borrow money from their landlords. In ability to pay off debts landed these people in a form of bonded slavery. The Commissioner of Scheduled Castes and Scheduled Tribes commented in his report of 1965-66: "The survey on the economic conditions of Paniyans of Wynad in Kerala conducted by the Bureau of Statistics and Economics of the Government of Kerala, throws light on the system of bonded labour prevalent in that area". Thus the ideologies of the naxalite revolutionaries appealed them most and the revolutionaries could garner a lot of support from these adivasis.

THE ROLE OF INTELLECTUALS

While 'comprador' bourgeoisie and nationalist bourgeoisie were despised in Charu Mazumdar's theories, the petty bourgeois was assigned a revolutionary role. Petty bourgeois are the middle and lower-middle class people consisting of teachers, white-collar employees, students etc. They had access to education and employment, and could thus afford an intellectual life free from the responsibility of production. This class played an important role in the political struggles during the British Rule. Impatient with the politics of compromise of the Indian National Congress led by the comprador-bourgeoisie, the radical section of this class turned to the path of armed revolt. Many of them later turned to communism. It is therefore no surprise that the intelligentsia came up to provide the naxalite movement with leadership and became its main ideologues.

It was these 'petty bourgeoisie' who provided the leadership for the naxalite revolts in Kerala also. In fact it was they who publicised the ideologies of Mao-TseTung and the Naxalbari incident among the peasants and the tribals. The important leaders among them were Kunnikkal Narayanan, Mandakini, T.V.Appu, Philip M. Prasad and Varghese. The daughter of Kunnikkal Narayanan and Mandakini, Ajitha, was also involved in the activities from her junior college days.

They were dissatisfied with the CPI(M) as the party did not advocate an armed revolution and was participating actively in the parliamentary democracy. They thought that after the death of Stalin, Soviet Union has given up the interests of world revolution and they saw China under Mao TseTung as the true adherents of Marxist principles. They used to listen to the Chinese Radio station Peking Radio which spread the message of Mao. And gradually they became the votaries of Chinese model of communism. Thus when after Naxalbari incident, Peking Radio broadcasted the editorial of 'People's Daily' showering praises on the Naxalbari peasants, these intellectuals decided to come up in support of the Naxalbari peasants.

They were dissatisfied with the revisionist policies of the Marxist party and the 'traitorous approach of the party leadership' in repressing the Naxalbari uprising. Thus they and many other members of the CPI(M) were embarrassed by and were critical of the first United Front Government's (of whom CPI(M) was in the cabinet) action against the Naxalbari rebels, left the party and were drawn to the Naxalite brand of Communism.

These intellectuals were mainly confined to the townships of Calicut and Thiruvananthapuram. They formed a coordination committee to spread the message of Naxalbari and published and distributed pamphlets and booklets containing the ideologies of Mao, whom they now began to see as their leader and their guide. They got these books about and by Mao from the Chinese Embassy itself. The Embassy even sent them photos and badges of Mao. It is this direct contact with the Chinese Government that helped the intellectual leaders in Kerala later to survive the wrath of the central leadership of CPI(ML) under Charu Mazumdar. They translated the works of Mao, which they got from the Chinese embassy, and published them in Malayalam under 'Rebel Publications'.

Thus their message of revolution spread widely in Kerala.

THE CHINESE CONTRIBUTION

As explained before, China provided all kind of support to the Indian Revolutionaries. The Chinese leaders, since 1967, seem to have taken upon themselves the task of directing and guiding the oncoming Indian Revolution. From the beginning of the 1966, Peking ideologues and propagandists have been formulating the theme of a mighty national revolutionary upsurge in India. With reports carefully culled from Indian newspapers and suitably edited, Peking Radio began to mount a continuing and ascending propaganda campaign against Congress rule in India.

So when peasants of Naxalbari rose in revolt, Peking found in it the signal it had been waiting for. Describing it as 'spring thunder over India', People's Daily held that it was the result of the militant action of the "revolutionaries" of the Indian Communist Party who had "deserted the united front government" in West Bengal because "it served as a tool of the Indian reactionaries. . . ." Encouraged by the outbreak of this peasant rebellion, the People's Daily laid down the Maoist line for India in clear, unmistakable terms. Naxalbari was the "prelude to a violent revolution by hundreds of millions of people throughout India "; but, to make it possible, the Indian revolution "must take the road of relying on the peasants, establishing base areas in the countryside, persisting in protracted armed struggle and using the countryside to encircle and finally capture the cities." The city-orientation of the Indian communist strategy must be given up and the peasants must be made "the invincible force of the Indian revolution "; the proletariat must therefore integrate with the peasants. Since the reactionary forces were "temporarily stronger than the revolutionary forces," communists must use "the whole set of the flexible strategy and tactics of people's war" and "persevere in protracted armed struggle." This armed struggle must begin in the countryside "where the reactionary rule is weak" and where "the revolutionaries can manoeuvre freely." It did not matter if the beginning was small, and if the peasants had to fight with bows and arrows;" so long as the Indian proletarian revolutionaries adhere to the revolutionary line of Marxism-Leninism, Mao Tse-tung's thought and rely on their great ally, the peasants, it is entirely possible for them to advance from one revolutionary rural base area to another in the huge backward rural areas and build a people's army of a new type."

And it is this propaganda of Peking Radio that inspired the revolutionaries in Kerala to start armed rebellions in the villages on the model of Naxalbari.

Immediate Causes for Early Revolts

The earliest of naxalite revolts was that in Pulpally-Thalassery. The Pulpally attack was directed against the exploitation of migrant farmers who had illegally occupied the forest land (about 20,000 acres) owned by Devaswom and were cultivating there for years. The forest department asked them to leave and filed criminal cases against them. A special Police Camp (M.S.P) was stationed there for the purpose of removing these migrants from these forest lands. The corruption and vulgarism of the police camped there antagonised these people. The Communist party, who promised to give title of the lands to these people during the elections also failed to deliver the promise. Therefore these people approached the bourgeoisie intellectuals who were spreading the ideology of Mao and Naxalbari to do something. These intellectuals, waiting for an opportunity to put their propaganda to practice, took up the issue.

The Thalassery attack was in support for the impoverished beedi workers of Kannur district. Their problems started with the 'Ganesh-Bharat Beedi crisis'. After coming to power, the E.M.S government implemented the beedi-cigar Rules as per the Minimum Wages Act. But the Ganesh and Bharat Beedi companies, which employed about 20,000 contractual labourers, were owned by proprietors in Mangalore (Karnataka District). So they closed down their operations in Kannur soon after the Act was implemented and shifted to Mangalore where the Act was not applicable. Thus more than 20,000 labourers lost their only means of livelihood. They began to work as agricultural labourers and thus the wages of the agricultural labourers also went down. The government couldn't solve this crisis. The naxalist idea was quite popular in this area and the naxalist leaders decided to take up the issue.

THE REVOLTS

Pulpally-Thalassery Revolts (Nov. 1968)

As mentioned earlier, Thalassery-Pulpally revolts was the first naxalite attack that took place in Kerala. The naxal leaders decided that they would synchronise the attacks in Pulpally and Thalassery. They formulated the plan that they would split into two. One group, under Kunnikkal Narayanan, would attack the Thalassery Police Station on 20th November and would procure arms from there. The other group, under Varghese, would then launch the attack in Pulppally and then both groups would rendezvous in the forests near Thirunelly after which they would launch a massive revolution in Thirunelly.

But the Thalassery attack turned out to be a complete failure. On the decided date, out of 1000 people expected, only 315 turned up. And out of those who turned up, many were panic-struck by the heavy security at the police station. So they decided not to attack the police station that night. Next evening, fewer people turned up, but nonetheless they went ahead in attacking the police station. But when the sentry at the police station rung the alarm, all but one fled, and the one grenade that was thrown at the station did not explode.

The other group was waiting in Pulpally for hearing about the news about Thalassery attack in the radio so as to launch their attack in Pulpally. They had formed a coordination council of which prominent members were Varghese, Thettamala Krishnan Kutti, 'Kurichiyan' Kunjiraman, Kisan Thomman, Philip M. Prasad and Ajitha. The council formulated the plan that they would attack the MSP camp followed by attack on Police Station and to destroy the records in registrar's office. They also decided to attack the houses of landlords on their way to Thirunelly.

But on the day of the attack, out of 400 people recruited from among the farmers and tribals only fifty turned up. They attacked the wireless camp and hacked the operator to death. They also attacked the Sub Inspector. Many had fled by this time. They decided not to attack the police station and Registrar's office. On their way to Thirunelly, they attacked the houses of two landlords and distributed the grains and money among the tribal people.

By this time, most of the people involved in Thalassery attack had been arrested by this police and none of their group came to the rendezvous point. So the group under Varghese had to wander through forests and finally when they reached Thirunelly, they were captured by the local people and were handed over to the Police.

Kuttiyadi Attack (1969)

Exactly one year after the Pulpally-Thalassery attack, those of early Naxalites who were outside the jail decided to attack Kuttiyadi Police station. They threw grenades at the station, destroyed the records and attacked the Sub Inspector. But when one of their leader Velayudhan was killed by the sentry fire, all fled after throwing the pamphlets titled 'Thalassery-Pulpally:one year'. The pamphlet concluded by saying that 'no force in the world can destroy the revolutionary spirit of the peasants of Kerala that sparked off the Thalassery-Pulpally revolts.'

Thirunelly Attack (1970)

Two months after Kuttiyadi police attack, the naxalite leader who led Pulpally-Thalassery also led another attack at Thirunelly. He was trying to mobilise the adivasis during this period. What happened in Thirunelly attack was personal vendetta. They murdered a landlord and a person whom they thought to be an agent of the police. They also looted another landlord's house.

The government was determined to curb naxalite menace by any force. The local police with the help of Central Reserve Police captured Varghese within few days and according to local people, was brutally murdered; though the police version was that he was killed in an encounter.

The police had arrested all the important naxalite leaders and the rest were dead by this time. And by 1976, the naxalite movement for all practical purposes died in Kerala. As the former Naxalite leader Ajitha put it, "I was caught by the police and landed in jail by the end of 1968. . . [I] remained in prison for nine years. When I came out of jail, the movement had faded away . . . circumstances were no longer conducive to revive the movement. So I chose to remain content with a mundane life".

On close examination, we can extract certain interesting features. One is that the revolts that happened in Kerala were not "a great storm of revolutionary armed struggle" as predicted by People's Daily, but were isolated events which happened after a long interval. In all the revolts, the attacks were directed against police stations. Naxalites attack police stations to symbolically represent their protest against the institutions of the state. But in Kerala, these attacks on police stations were not symbolic, they were the end.

Another interesting feature is the number of people that participated in these revolts. Even after months of campaigning, propaganda and recruitment, the naxalite leaders could mobilise only very few people into the struggle. It is also important to note that it is the local population which captured the naxalite leaders and handed over them to the Police.

Fails to take Roots

In most of the histories written about naxalist movement in India, the naxalite revolts that happened in Kerala are hardly mentioned. Even a Keralite author K. Panoor who wrote a travelogue about Naxalbari maintains in his book that in Kerala also 'smokes' of naxalite revolts could be seen. Prakash Karat maintains, 'It [the naxalite movement] petered out at an early stage, never having achieved any coherent ideological organisational content'.

Why did Naxalism as a movement fail to take roots in Kerala? Did the naxalite revolts that happened had any significance? The researcher in this chapter attempts to find an answer to these difficult questions.

On careful analysis, we can find a number of reasons why naxalism fizzled out at an early stage in Kerala. One very important reason was that the social and political situation prevailing in Kerala was not conducive for the fostering of revolutionist ideas of Naxalism which attempts to overthrow the basic institutions and assumptions of the government. As a prominent early naxalite K. Venu said, and as several former members often claim, "the naxalites [in Kerala] failed to realise the realities of Kerala and the impact of the progressive policies followed by successive democratic (especially Left) governments and, before them, other enlightened rulers. They failed to understand that the driving force of armed struggle as envisaged by Charu Mazumdar - the class rivalry of poor, landless peasants against the landlords - was already satiated to an extent in Kerala through social reforms, (though imperfect) land reforms, the crumbling of the landlord-tenant link, the organisation of the working class and the spread of literacy that made old-world-style exploitation impossible".

The government was determined to curb naxalism completely by following a 'carrot and stick'-a policy of carrot towards the people and a policy of stick towards naxalites. Soon after the Pulpally incident, government gave titles of land to the migrant farmers and started 'Dinesh' beedi company to give employment to the unemployed workers. The state government led by Communist party passed Kerala Scheduled Tribes (Restriction on Transfer of Lands and Restoration of Alienated Lands) Act in 1975 with a view to appease and wean away adivasis from the naxalites.

While the government followed a policy of appeasement towards farmers and adivasis, they resorted to extreme repressive measures towards the naxalites. The police arrested almost all the leaders of the movement. The police offensive played a very significant role in curbing the naxalite movement in Kerala.

An essential condition for the success of armed rebellions of the type envisaged by naxalism is the rapid expansion of the rural bases and the fighting forces of the revolutionaries.[17] But as we have seen, in Kerala, the naxalite leaders, mostly belonging to the 'petty bourgeoisie' class, were not able to mobilise large sections of farmers or adivasis. The movement failed to advance beyond the initial stages of the warfare-attacks on police station, attacks on class enemies etc. and that too these were carries out in a few pockets of power. No programmes with long term goals were chalked out and one is tempted to ask what the naxalites planned to achieve with this individual and isolated acts of violence.

Yet another reason for the failure of the movement is that military requirements of the movement were neglected by the leadership. There was a lack of military experience and training which is highly essential for this kind of movement.[18] Moreover, they disregarded the military strength of the enemy.

None of the attacks were planned and coordinated which led to dissensions and pandemonium.

Another very important reason for the early death of the naxalite movement in Kerala was the disunity among the naxalites from the very early stage. The early naxalites did not have the support of the AICCCR. In April 1969, soon after the formation of the all-India coordination committee of the Communist Party of India (Marxist- Leninist) under Charu Mazumdar, a State organising committee of the CPI(M-L) was constituted in Kerala under the leadership of Ambadi Sankarankutty Menon. The imposition of an "unpopular" leadership by the central committee was a fact that led to the first of the divisions within the movement in the State. Again, the leaders where divided into different groups. Thus while Kunnikkal Narayanan's group sought direct actions, there were other groups stumbling along in different directions. There was one group at Trichur and Calicut, another at Trivandrum headed by the city's ex-Mayor, Kosal Ramdas, and yet a third led by K.P.R Gopalan, trying to coordinate the activities of all these groups.the activities of all these groups were, however, confined to publishing Maoist articles in different journals.

On a final analysis, the researcher is of the opinion that the conditions prevailing in Kerala was not conducive for the growth of naxalist ideas and therefore the movement died a natural death.

SUMMING UP

It was pointed out that the revolts which drew its inspirations from the much publicised Naxalbari revolt were led by the 'petty bourgeoisie' class. These people within the Marxist party had shifted their loyalty to Communist China and Mao. So when Peking Radio, which was the main propagandist instrument of the Communist China, praised the Naxalbari revolt and called upon the communists to organise similar revolts all over the country, the revolutionaries within the Marxist party in Kerala also decided to organise armed rebellions on the lines of Naxalbari.

But we could see that the same mistakes which made Naxalbari rebellion a failure-failure to advance beyond the initial stages of warfare, disunity among the ranks, lack of military skills and training- was repeated in the revolts which happened in Kerala. The stringent measures adopted by the government to deal with the revolutionaries prevented the movement from taking roots. The government were also successful in appeasing the local population to an extent and could prevent them from going in the 'naxalbari' way.

But more than anything else, the class contradictions within the Kerala Society was not high as to spark off an armed rebellion. People posed their faith in the democratically elected governments and the progressive policies followed by them. The revolutionaries failed to grasp this reality of the Kerala society. As to the question whether there is a future for the naxalite movement, the following excerpt is very apt: "The crucial condition of the future success of the Naxalites, is a new broad-based socialist movement with new organisational strategies, to which they could contribute, and which would carry them forward into a wider political arena where they could begin to act out their politics with patience and understanding. But before that they need to make peace among themselves".

Issues and State Response

Communism may have died in Europe but its violent manifestation has been haunting India in the form of Naxalism. Its appeal among the dispossessed and underprivileged rural poor in several parts, especially the east and south-east part of India, at times referred to as the Red Corridor is very much binding. The rural poor see in this movement a hope to free themselves from their present miserable conditions.

The police and bureaucrats of at least eight Indian states (Bihar, West Bengal, Maharashtra, Madhya Pradesh, Chhattisgarh, Jharkhand, Andhra Pradesh and Orissa, which comprise a large chunk of the Indian land mass, and accounts for more than half of the Indian population), meet at regular intervals to devise ways and means to check the armed guerillas who operate in a narrow belt of Naxalite pockets that stretches across these states.

Under the leadership of Charu Mazumdar, the naxalites defined the objective of the movement as 'seizure of power through an agrarian revolution'. Their strategy was to replace the old feudal order with one, which would implement land reforms, and to free the poor from the clutches of landlords. They adopted guerilla warfare as the tactics to achieve their objective. They visualized 'liberation' of territories and they thus hoped to set up 'liberated zones' gradually in different parts of the country that would eventually coalesce into a territorial unit under Naxalite hegemony.

The police suppressed the Naxalbari uprising within a few months. Despite this, Naxalism as an ideology kept growing and is today a force to reckon with in at least 13 states in India. Suppression, oppression and exploitation are generally said to be the real reason behind the exceptional growth and support of the naxalism.

THE BACKGROUND

The rise of Naxalism in India has some definite connection with the contemporary global scenario of 1960s. After the Second World War, intellectuals around the world were looking at the new world order afresh. This was the period, when new radicalism was breaking out, marked by the re-reading of Marx, the rediscovery of the sources of revolutionary humanism and the revival of the ideals that inspired individual courage and the readiness to sacrifice for a cause. It was like a mini renaissance. These trends were reflected in the national liberation struggle of the Vietnamese people, in the anti-war movements in North America, in the students' agitations in Western Europe, in Che Guevara's self-sacrifice in the jungles of Bolivia in pursuit of the old dream of international solidarity of all revolutionaries, and in China's Cultural. Also, this was the period when Jawaharlal Nehru, Nasser and Tito were suggesting alternative of the two power blocks in the shape of the Non-Aligned Movement. So, intellectual warfare was already on and this has just uplifted the thought of Indian communists also, who started to look at the peasants, workers' plight in the newly found beacon. With such developments in backyard, Naxalism initially began as a campaign for putting an end to bureaucratic authoritarianism and transforming the individual. The Naxalite leaders drew inspiration from the Indian peasant jacqueries of the18th and 19th centuries (which were directed against the British colonialists and their Indian landed agents), and the more modern organized armed peasants' struggles led by Communists in Telengana in south India in the late 1940s, as well as the contemporary Vietnamese war of liberation and other global demonstrations of protest.

Originating in a small village of West Bengal, the Naxalite ideology gained rapid currency in other parts of West Bengal and India within a few years. By the early 1970s, the Naxalite movement had spread from far-flung areas like Andhra Pradesh and Kerala in the south, to Bihar in the east, and Uttar Pradesh and Punjab in the north. And, on April 22, 1969, the Communist Party of India (Marxist-Leninist) was formed when the entire state units of UP and Jammu and Kashmir and considerable sections in Bihar and Andhra Pradesh came together. For some time the naxalite guerillas had virtually set up alternative administrative machinery in Srikakulam in Andhra Pradesh, to which they referred to as 'liberated zone'. In parts of Bihar and Uttar Pradesh, the Naxalites succeeded in mobilizing the peasantry to recover lands that they had lost to the moneylender-cum-landlord class (to whom they had mortgaged their properties in lieu of money) and carry their harvested crops to their homes. In Punjab rich landlords and policemen were targeted by bands of Naxalites. In Midnapur and Birbhum of West Bengal armed peasants' struggle broke out. Incidentally, in Andhra Pradesh and in West Bengal, the Naxalites found their main support among the aboriginal tribal communities, who had been the most oppressed and marginalized in Indian society—the Girijans in Andhra Pradesh and the Santhals in West Bengal.

The naxalbari movement was going so strong at that time that the government of India decided to set up a committee to look into the matter. The committee submitted its report, entitled, The Causes and Nature of Current Agrarian Tensions, wherein it was said that the basic cause of unrest was the defective implementation of laws enacted to protect the interests of the tribals. The government was also worried over the law and order situation in the areas of naxal influence. So, government took strong steps against the naxalites. By 1972, the government had succeeded in defeating the Naxalite rebellion to some extent. Charu Mazumdar was captured from a Calcutta hideout in July 1972. Mazumdar died in police custody 12 days after his arrest, raising suspicions about the treatment meted out to him by the police. And, by 1973, the number of Naxalite activists and supporters held in different jails all over India had swelled. Naturally, the allegation of the ill-treatment meted to the detainees was made by left wing politicians and scholars. Noam Chomsky and Simone de Beauvoir signed a note protesting against the Indian government's approach and sent it to New Delhi on August 15, 1974. The emergency clamped on India by Indira Gandhi on June 26, 1975 was a major attempt at curtailing the growing influence of naxalism. Almost all the elite as well as ground level leaders of the movement were either in jails or had gone underground leading to weakening of the movement.

INTRODUCTION

Naxalite is an informal name given to the groups that represent revolutionary communists born out of a split in the Indian communist movement on Chinese and Soviet lines, wherein Chinese ideology dominates. And, Naxalism is the ideology that these revolutionaries harbour and advocate. The term owes its origin to Naxalbari, a small village in West Bengal, where 49-year old Charu Mazumdar and Kanu Sanyal of Communist Party of India (Marxist) led a militant peasant uprising in 1967. Their aim was to build a "revolutionary opposition" in order to establish "revolutionary rule" in India. Hugely influenced by Mao Zedong of China, Charu Mazumdar advocated that the peasants and lower classes must overthrow the government and upper classes, that he thought, were responsible for the unenviable plight.

Breaking away from the CPI (M), these Naxalites organized the All India Coordination Committee of Communist Revolutionaries (AICCCR). Now, peasants' uprisings were organized in several parts of the country. In 1969 AICCCR gave birth to Communist Party of India (Marxist-Leninist). But, pretty soon the naxal movement had to bear with two major jolts, one was the revolt of Satyanarayan Singh in 1971 and the second was the death of Charu Mazumdar, the very next year. These two incidents caused fragmentation in the ranks of naxalism. But the significant fact is that almost all the Naxalite groups trace their origin to the CPI (ML).

However, Maoist Communist Centre has always maintained a separate tendency. It has evolved from the southern group, generally called among the Maoist circle of India as Dakshin Desh-group. Now MCC is a banned organization in India but it has fused with People's War Group and the fusion is known as the Communist Party of India (Maoist).

Another tendency in the naxalite movement in India is that of the Andhra revolutionary communists, which is mainly presented by UCCRI (ML), following the mass line legacy of T. Negi Reddy.

However all the naxalite groups are not militant in character and today some groups have become legal organizations participating in parliamentary elections. Communist Party of India (Marxist-Leninist) Liberation is one such important organization. On the other hand Communist Party of India (Maoist) and Communist Party of India (Marxist-Leninist, Janashakti), are engaged in armed guerrilla struggles. Typically, there is a groundswell of public support for such activities, though it seems to have come down in recent years with counter-movements such as those led by Mahendra Karma becoming popular.

The cause of the peasants and the fact that naxalism identifies itself with poor people's cause and aspirations, it has become popular among intellectuals and even movie makers alike. Several movies relating to the Naxal movement have been made, such as Lal Salaam, Jukti Takko Aar Tappo, and very recently Hazaaron Khwaishen Aisi and Hazaar Chaurasi Ki Maa. There are also some pro-Maoist literaturists like Mr. Pendyala Varavara Rao. Mr Varavara Rao is originally Telugu literaturist and some of his books have been translated into Hindi.

NEW PHASES

For some time it seemed that naxalism would die in India but it entered a new phase, when Emergency was lifted and a new government came into power at the center after 1977 general elections. The Janata Party government released naxalite leaders from jails following a wide scale movement organized by various human rights groups in India and abroad.

In the changed political situation, which many socialists described as the second Independence (after 1947), the different naxalite factions found an opportunity to chart out a fresh course of action in the light of past experiences. Though they remained committed to their original objective of replacing the feudal order with one based on social equality but they differed hugely on the question of tactics.

The divide was so sharp that the factions parted their ways. One faction (like the Liberation group of the CPI - M-L, concentrated in Bihar) decided to go along the parliamentary path of struggle by participating in elections and thereby bringing forth the desired changes in the economic and socio-political set up of the country. While the others, like the People's War Group (PWG) in Andhra Pradesh, and Maoist Communist Centre (MCC) in Bihar preferring to go back to the path of guerilla warfare. During the last two decades since the 1980s, these two different streams of the Naxalite movement drifted along with their respective tactics, often fighting among themselves.

However, in the recent past the armed naxalite groups have emerged as the main challenge to the governance in India. These groups have only expanded their influence area and recent trends show marked improvement in their strength. They have now spread from their old pockets in West Bengal, Bihar and Andhra Pradesh to new guerilla zones in Orissa, Maharashtra, Chhattisgarh, Jharkhand, Madhya Pradesh and Uttar Pradesh. So, they have come out stronger in the new millennium.

Significantly the main support base of the naxlas in the new areas are the same poorest and the most deprived classes, the landless and tribal people who have been or are being ousted from their homes by up-coming industrial projects, or being denied access to their traditional forest resources, and who continue to suffer from non-availability of education, employment and health facilities in their far-flung and inaccessible villages.

In the era of globalized or multinational communication the modern manifestations of naxal movement, too, have gone the international way. Hence, the organizations like, PWG, MCC etc have established a network with similar revolutionary organizations in Nepal, Bangladesh, Bhutan and Sri Lnaka under the aegis of the Coordination Committee of Maoist Parties and Organizations of South Asia (CCMPOSA). Moreover, all these South Asian Maoist organizations and parties are also members of an international organization called the Revolutionary Internationalist Movement (RIM). Recently, in 2003 the representatives of the various naxalite groups met in India to chalk out strategy.

However, one thing is pretty obvious at this point of time that the naxalites do not control any significant portion of land within the territory of India, notwithstanding their claim of the so-called 'liberated zone'. And, with the genuine redressal of the land related problems in the affected areas would definitely ease the crisis.

GOVERNMENT POLICY

While tabling the status report on the naxal problems in March 2006, the Union Home Minister Shivraj Patil outlined the 14-point strategy to deal with the naxal problems in India. The report deals in following policy matters mainly:

1. He conceded that naxalism is not merely a law & order problem, therefore the Government should address this menace simultaneously on political security, development and public perception management fronts in a holistic manner.
2. Acknowledging naxalism as an inter-state problem, the report says that the states will have to adopt a collective approach and pursue a coordinated response to counter it.
3. The report also emphasizes that the states need to improve police response and pursue effective and sustained police action against naxalites and their infrastructure individually and jointly.
4. The Union government categorically said in the report that there would be no peace dialogue by the affected

states with the naxal groups unless the latter agree to give up violence and arms.

5. Outlining the importance of meaningful political involvement of the affected populace in the mainstream politics the report asks the political parties to strengthen their cadre base in naxsal affected areas so that the potential youth there can be weaned away from the path of naxal ideology.
6. The report asks to adopt an approach with special focus on accelerated sociw-economic development of the backward areas by ensuring the regular involvement of NGOs, intelligentsia, civil liberties groups etc. to minimize over ground support for the naxalite ideology and activity in the affected areas.
7. The government now focuses now on the efficient use of the Mass media to highlight the futility of naxal violence and loss of life and property caused by it and developmental schemes of the Government in the affected areas so as to restore people's faith and confidence in the Government machinery.
8. The report also says that there is an urgent need of according higher priority by the state government to the faster socio-economic development in the affected areas within the territory of the respective states. The focus sareas should be to distribute land to the landless poor as part of the speedy implementation of the land reforms, ensure development of physical infrastructure like roads, communication, power etc. and provide employment opportunities to the youth in these areas.

GOVERNMENT MEASURES

1. The government has emphasized on the modernization of State Police force. Funds are given to the States under the Police Modernization Scheme to modernize their police forces in terms of modern weaponry, latest communication equipment, mobility and other infrastructure. The naxal-affected States have also been asked to identify vulnerable police stations and

outposts in the naxal areas and take up their fortification under the Scheme.

2. The Security Related Expenditure (SRE) Scheme of February 2005 has been revised. The level of reimbursement under the Scheme has been raised from 50% to 100% and new items like insurance scheme for police personnel, community policing, rehabilitation of surrendered naxalites, expenditure incurred on publicity to counter propaganda of naxalites, other security related items not covered under the Police Modernization Scheme etc., have been covered. The Scheme also allows release of funds to the naxal-affected States as advance.
3. The state governments are being supplied the Mine Protected Vehicles under the Police Modernization Scheme to counter the land mine/IED attacks.
4. In order to supplement the efforts of the States in providing an effective response to the naxal violence, Central Para Military Forces have been deployed on a long-term basis as requested by the affected States.
5. The naxal-affected States have been sanctioned India Reserve (IR) battalions mainly to strengthen security apparatus at their level as also to enable the States to provide gainful employment to the youth, particularly in the naxal areas. The States have been asked to expedite raising of these battalions.
6. In order to ensure that the Maoists of Nepal do not get in touch with the Indian naxalites the SSB has been given the responsibility to guard the Indo-Nepal border with special care towards this.
7. The government has revised the recruitment guidelines to divert the youth from the naxal-affected areas to get into government jobs. Now, it has been permitted that 40% of the total recruitment in the Central Para Military Force (CRPF) can be taken up from the naxal or militancy affected areas.
8. Another important measure of the government is related to the backward district development. The Central Government has provided financial assistance of Rs. 2,475 crores for 55 naxal affected districts in the

9 States of Andhra Pradesh, Bihar, Chhattisgarh, Orissa, Jharkhand, Maharashtra, Madhya Pradesh, Uttar Pradesh & West Bengal under the Backward Districts Initiative (BDI) component of the Rsahtriya Sam Vikas Yojana (RSVY).

9. The government has requested the Planning Commission to include other naxal affected areas under their proposed Scheme of Backward Regions Grant Funds (BRGF) for which an outlay of Rs. 5,000 crores has been set apart from 2005-06 fiscal year onwards.
10. The naxal problem has a very deep connection with the tribal and forested areas as even today the main base of the naxal movement comes from these places only. In order to address the areas of disaffection among the tribals, the government is making efforts on the legislation front also and the recognizing the right of the forest dwellers on the forest produces is an attempt to win over the tribals against the naxalites.
11. Since their beginning the naxal groups have been raising land and livelihood related issues mainly. So the central government now pushing the states to carry the land reforms as fast as possible. But land reforms in India has not been a political issue only rather a social and prestige issue also, so, it always seems difficult for the state governments to carry out any such legislative measures for the fear of losing vital middle class' support. The States have also been asked to put greater attention on creating employment opportunities in the naxal affected areas with special focus on creation of physical infrastructure in terms of roads, communication, power as also social infrastructure such as schools, hospitals, etc.

To do all this the strategy of the government right now emphasizes on:

(i) To strengthen intelligence set-up at the state level;
(ii) To pursue effective and sustained intelligence driven police action against naxalites and their infrastructure individually and jointly by the states.

(iii) To accelerate development in the naxal affected areas.

STATUS OF NAXALISM

Since 1980 clashes between police and Naxalite Maoist revolutionaries have taken place in various parts of India with majority of incidents taking place in northwestern Andhra Pradesh. In some areas, though very small in expanse, the naxalites dispense summary justice in "people's courts" which in some cases condemn to death suspected police informers, village headmen, and others deemed to be "class enemies" or "caste oppressors". Over the past few years, hundreds of policemen and suspected Naxalites have been killed, according to press reports and human rights organization.

However, the human rights groups allege that "encounters" are usually faked by the police to cover up the torture and subsequent murder of Naxalite suspects, sympathizers, or informers. Andhra police have formed an armed vigilant group known as the "Green Tigers", whose mission is to combat Naxalite groups in the state. The area under naxal influence has been on increase and right now even with conservative statistics 76 districts in 9 States are affected by naxalite activity/influence in varying degrees. It has been reported that CP(Maoist) is trying to establish a 'Compact Revolutionary Zone' (CRZ) spreading from Nepal through Bihar and the Dandakaranya region to Andhra Pradesh.

The Union government on March 13, 2006 tabled the status report on the problems of naxalism in India. Here, the government accepts that the naxalite movement continues to persist in terms of spatial spread, intensity of violence, militarization and consolidation, ominous linkages with subversive/secessionist groups and increased efforts to elicit mass support.

Identifying the problem the status chapter says that the naxalites operate in vacuum created by absence of administrative and political institutions, espouse the local demands and take advantage of the disenchantment prevalent among the exploited segments of the population and seek to offer an alternative system of governance which promises emancipation of these segments from the clutches of 'exploiter' classes through the barrel of a gun.

As per the report the naxalite violence has claimed 669 lives including 153 police personnel in 1594 incidents in 2005 as against 556 casualties in 1533 incidents in 2004. The report also says that the quantum of naxal violence has shown a marginal increase of about 4% in 2005 (over 2004), while resultant casualties have however, gone up by 18.1%.

The report also talks about the incidents of naxal violence in 2006 and it says that in the current year (till February) while the number of incidents of naxal violence has decreased by 29% over the corresponding period of 2005 (246 incidents as against 347 in 2005). But, civilian and security forces casualties have increased by 11.4% (116 as against 104 in 2005). However, such incidents have seen marked increase in number and impact of late particularly since June.

The report says that the substantial increase in naxal violence and deaths in Andhra Pradesh can be attributed to the unilateral withdrawal by naxalites from the peace talks in January 2005 and consequent stepped up violence by them. In Chhattisgarh, resistance being put up by the Salva Judum (anti-naxal movement by people) activists and the efforts of the security forces to dislodge the naxalites from their strongholds are the main reasons for increased violence and resultant deaths.

The status report also acknowledges that while the States of Bihar and Jharkhand have recorded decrease in naxal violence in 2005, a few high profile incidents like looting of weapons from the Giridih Home Guard training centre on 11-11-2005 in Jharkhand and the jailbreak on 13-11-2005 in Jehanabad, Bihar, have taken place in recent months.

WHY NAXALISM ALIVE?

It was under the land-to-the-tiller slogan that naxalism developed in West Bengal despite the fact that land reforms have been among the proclaimed priority of the government at both state and union levels, and that the very first amendment to the constitution was made to serve this end. But at the same time it must be conceded that land reform as a state objective has disappeared from Indian policy-making in the age of economic liberalization has not only kept the Naxalite agenda alive, rather has given it intellectual and numerical strength.

All the governmental programmes of alleviating poverty have not procuced the desired results and even today government policies do not seem to focus on the problem so seriously. The NDA government's Food-for-Work programme or the UPA's Employment Guarantee Programme hardly meet the basic demand for land rights in rural India. Even the so-called backward caste political flavour has not made any difference to the ground situation. The evidence comes from the political games that have been so obvious in Bihar and Uttar Pradesh.

It was under the land-to-the-tiller slogan that naxalism developed in West Bengal despite the fact that land reforms have been among the proclaimed priority of the government at both state and union levels, and that the very first amendment to the constitution was made to serve this end. But at the same time it must be conceded that land reform as a state objective has disappeared from Indian policy-making in the age of economic liberalization has not only kept the Naxalite agenda alive, rather has given it intellectual and numerical strength.

All the governmental programmes of alleviating poverty have not procuced the desired results and even today government policies do not seem to focus on the problem so seriously. The NDA government's Food-for-Work programme or the UPA's Employment Guarantee Programme hardly meet the basic demand for land rights in rural India. Even the so-called backward caste political flavour has not made any difference to the ground situation. The evidence comes from the political games that have been so obvious in Bihar and Uttar Pradesh.

The apparent rise of the backward castes to the political helm in these states might look like strengthening the democratic trends in India but it definitely has had the paradoxical effect of freezing land relations. They always advocated the cause and concern of the deprived and oppressed ones in the society but never really did they enact anything that could have changed the material status of the class they have been getting support from.

This has also been realized by the naxalites and they have just encashed the fallacy of the so-called advocates of the oppressed and deprived ones. The result is increase in strength of the naxalite even in the era of globalization.

Another aspect that is linked to the spread of the naxalites in the hilly terrain of India extending from Bihar to Andhra Pradesh is a conscious decision by the naxalites to take up the issues affecting the tribal people of these regions. With popular back up the naxalites know that they can make any government to listen to their demands. And, by first taking up their problems the naxalites lure them to their cadre and then initiate them to their ideology.

India's quest for development has caused apart from other things, the commercialization of forest resources, thereby reducing the traditional right and access of the tribal inhabitants to the forested areas, which are still considered as their original homes of the tribal people. Moreover, the transfer of tribal land to the non-tribal people despite several legal strictures continues unabated. Mining, construction, dams, and many other developmental activities have caused large scale displacement of the tribals, who anyways love their own environment due historical and cultural factors.

So, there has been a readymade resentment among the tribal populace and it could easily serve as a fertile ground for popularization of any anti-government or anti-mainstream ideology. The naxalites have realized this quite clearly and so they have been able to establish a good ground level support base in these areas. A central Naxalite agenda also includes tribal self-determination, that is, asserting the rights of the tribals over local resources.

Though the government has several tribal development programmes aimed at overall progress of the people and the regions. But, it seems that all these programmes collectively have created an elite among the tribal population itself, leading to increased resentment among the tribals. The problem has been compounded by the massive out-migration due to increased poverty and income gap in the tribal society.

The UPA government has introduced a bill in the parliament for safeguarding the land rights of the locals in the tribal areas is a good move but it's a late one. Similarly the extension of the Panchayati Raj programmes to tribal areas by giving greater power to the tribal village assembly is a modest measure in the right direction, but unless structural deformities are addressed in proper manner and the measures are undertaken to restore rights over land and forest, there is every possibility that the Panchayati Raj structures would continue to be manipulated by local elites. And, with this there remains every single chance of disaffection among the rural and tribal populace, which would keep naxalism alive in India.

TRENDS AND DEVELOPMENT

In 2005, naxal violence has been reported from 509 police stations in 11 states which works out to 5.8% of the total number of police station in these states. Available reports, however, suggest that CPI (Maoists) have been trying to increase their influence and act in parts of Kamataka, Kerala, Tamil Nadu and Uttranchal and also in new areas in some of the already affected states.

After the merger of CPML-PW and MCCI into CPI (Maoist) in September, 2004, they are reported to be trying to woo other splinter groups and have also consolidated their front organizations into 'Revolution Democratic Front' (RDF) to intensify their mass contact programme. Fresh recruitment of cadres is also reported. Indian naxalite groups continue to sustain their fraternal and logistic links with Nepalese Maoists, though there are no strategic and operational likes between the two.

The latest tactics adopted by the naxal outfits are to engage in simultaneous multiple attacks in large numbers particularly against police forces and police establishments. This has led to increased casualties of police personnel in 2005 mainly due to IED/landmine blasts by the naxalites. A total of 153 police personnel have laid down their lives in 2005 in 194 attacks by naxalites on the police as against 100 in 232 such attacks in 2004.

EFFECTS ON ECONOMY

The Naxalite rebellion, has festered for more than three decades in India's countryside. Notwithstanding the fact that the struggle is taking place far from Delhi's glitzy new suburbs or Bangalore's booming technology hub, its effects are increasingly being felt across India.

The Prime Minister of India, Manmohan Singh, recently referred to the Naxal insurgency problem as, "the single biggest internal-security challenge ever faced by our country".

Despite the long-time presence of the insurgency problem within India the state has taken woefully limited measures to counter the problem. Potentially the most catastrophic effect that the insurgency can have on the country is on its energy resources. Most of the energy rich sectors of the country fall under the areas dominated by Naxalites.

The Maoists campaign against the government will have far-reaching consequences on India's stability and, most particularly, its energy security. It is an alarming fact that the Naxalite insurgency is strongest precisely in the areas with the richest natural resources, especially the coal that is the power behind the Indian economy.

The state of Chattisgarh is by far the worst effected with the Naxal problem. To make matters worse, the state is generously endowed with rich minerals and other naturals resources. Forest accounts fpr 46% of the total land area. Sal and teak are the main trees of the forests both of which have high economical value. Timber accounts for 40% of the total revenue from the forest sector. Chattisgarh is home to 28 varieties of major minerals including Bauxite, Garnet, Quartz, Aluminium Diamond and Gold. In addition, the state produces all the tin ore in India and is renowned for having one of the best iron ore deposits the world over.

The Naxalites have a presence in almost half of India's 28 states, while in some of the poorer and most heavily tribal states, particularly Chhattisgarh, Andhra Pradesh, Orissa, Jharkand and West Bengal, they have turned into a political force to reckon with. These five states account for about 85% of India's coal resources, and continued disruption and deterioration of the political environment could lead to profound consequences for both India and its neighbours.

Coal is an important part of the Indian Economy as it accounts for about 55% of India's current primary energy supply and 75% of its electricity generation. A prolonged or excessively costly resource war in these states could cripple the economy and alter the global import balance if India has to look elsewhere for energy resources.

Recent months, has seen an upsurge in the number of direct attacks by Naxalite rebels on the energy industry. Naxalites recently killed coal-mine security officers in Chhattisgarh and burned vehicles from a coal-survey team, The Mineral Exploration Corp of India. In the coal-rich region of Andhra Pradesh, Naxalites are known to destroy vast quantities of mining equipment.

The threat posed by the Naxalite's energy-related violence is expanding. India's Oil and Natural Gas Co. has dramatically beefed up security at its facilities in Jharkand and other Naxal sensitive areas in response to warnings from government officials about Naxalite attacks.

Chhattisgarh's government last year signed almost US$3 billion in agreements to build power plants and other energy-related infrastructure. But such agreements would hang in the balance if the violence does not cease. Naxalites frequently levy their own "taxes" on resource extraction in districts within their control while many ideological Naxalites are opposed to the development of additional coalmines and power plants at any price.

The rebel groups control much of the countryside, where according to numerous accounts by locals, they in essence run a parallel government and administration. The local newspapers are filled daily with accounts of fatal battles between Naxalites and government forces. Government officials have not visited parts of many districts for years in fear of their lives.

The Naxalite insurgency is creating hurdles in India's economic growth story. The international financial services company, Citigroup Inc, addressing the security problem said that the Naxalite insurgency could not only hamper India's economic growth but also restrict the in-flow of Foreign Direct Investment into the country. The country is facing four main challenges such as higher infrastructure spends, overcoming the human resource paradigm, a need for inclusive growth and politics including the Maoist challenge.

Naxalite movement against industrialization has become a looming risk and acts as a deterrent to larger companies. The Naxals have also issued a direct threat to various multinational corporations to stop developmental work in the state who see the hi-tech industries as a symptom of an oppressive capitalist system.

Fear of being caught in the cross-fire between the Maoists and the state law officers has forced over 3000 villagers in the Naxal controlled region of Andhra Pradesh to refuse telephone connections. The villagers fear that they would be caught between the two warring parties if they apply for phone connections. Either the Maoists would suspect them of being police informers or the cops would label as Maoist sympathisers refusing to pass on information.

In Chhattisgarh, one of the hotbeds of the Naxal insurgency, around 1800 villages are bereft of telecommunication facilities. Karnataka which seems to be the next of the Maoist rebels may soon face the same predicament. Another reason that discourages phone usage is the frequent attacks by the rebels on telephone exchanges. Telephone exchanges are the second most favourite targets of the Maoists after police stations. A total of 270 exchanges have been attacked so far with Andhra Pradesh accounting for 265. The damage caused by these attacks ranges anywhere from Rs.30,000 to Rs. 50 lakh.

Each time the Maoists attack a telephone exchange, they not only succeed in cutting off all lines of communication but also scare people about the repercussions of using these utilities.

The movement could pose a threat to governance and could hinder investment flows if not restricted in time.

The intensifying civil war in parts of India's countryside will have profound effects not just for India's energy security, but for the global economy as well. The growing unrest will bear close scrutiny over the coming months. Continued deterioration in security levels in India's coal heartland could have a significant impact on energy security in India and beyond.

INTERNATIONAL CONNECTIONS

The Indian Maoists have been emboldened by the recent success of their Nepalese counterparts, who have emerged as a legitimate power center after a decade of protracted people's war. The effects are already visible in Bihar, where despite complex security arrangement by the state police, partial success of a bandh in October 2006, by the indicated that they are capable enough to strike a crippling blow to the administration. The 24-hour bandh was called by the CPI-M in Bihar, Jharkhand, Orissa and Chhattisgarh from Oct. 29, 2006-midnight to Oct. 30, 2006-midnight.

Bihar is a fertile ground for the breeding of Naxalites due to poor governance, complex social structure, chronic poverty and formation of private armies. The Naxalites under the banner of the MCC (Maoist Communist Centre) and PW (People's War) are currently active in over 33 of Bihar's 38 districts. In addition, Nepalese Maoists make their presence felt in the State taking advantage of the 700 kilometers of porus border between the two neighbouring countries. Despite efforts by the security personnel manning the border, it is not possible to effectively check the movements of the Nepalese Maoists because of forests and inhospitable terrain that account for much of the border area. Northern Bihar districts are facing a spurt in Maoist violence ever since the Maoists have become active in Nepal.

As India struggles to come to terms with a difficult internal security situation in the wake of continuing Maoist attacks, the 'United Front' effort by the Asian Maoist outfits in general and linkages between the Nepalese Maoists and its Indian counterparts in particular are a grave cause of concern for India. In addition, internal security is in constant threat due to ideological, strategic and organisational linkages between the CPI-Maoist and the CPN-Maoist.

The ripples of any development in the Maoist movement in Nepal are felt in India as well. A document condemning the moderate approach and stating its disadvantages to the furthering of the Maoist movement in Andhra Pradesh was circulated among the Indian cadres. In a general consensus it was felt that the party should have followed the 'militant' line as practised by the Maoists in Nepal and the LTTE in Sri Lanka.

A document of the CPI (Maoist) titled "New Challenges: Our Perspectives", meant for internal circulation, emphasised the need for an evaluation of the developments of events on the Indian front, and, then redefine its strategies and field tactics accordingly. The Indian Maoists are closely following the chain of events in Nepal and monitoring the actions the actions of their Nepalese counterparts. The Maoist victory in Nepal along with the modernization of its weaponry by procuring new and sophisticated weapons has strengthened the morale of the Indian rebels and encouraged them to accelerate their insurgent activities in India.

While the Maoists in India are ready to start a United Front with the support of its South Asian counter parts, the state responses to the menace is incoherent and laid-back. Even the formation of Naxalite Coordination Committee and Task Force comprising officers of the nine Naxal-affected states have failed to generate a coordinated effort among the administration of the Naxal effected states. Apart from the so-called multi-pronged action against the Maoists, the authorities are reluctant to take further steps to check external influence over the Naxals.

Many Indian insurgent groups, most notably the United Liberation Front of Assam and the CPI –M lend a helping hand to the Communist Party of Nepal (CPN). Expatriate Nepalese living in India provide funds and support for the CPN.

The first signs of contact between the Maoists of the neighboring countries was reportedly registered during 1989-1990, when the two groups started collaborating in order to expand their area of influence. Subsequently, they began the process of building up what is now known as the Revolutionary Corridor extending from Nepal across six Indian States, including Bihar, Chhattisgarh, Jharkhand, Andhra Pradesh, Orissa and Madhya Pradesh. This area came to be called the Compact Revolutionary Zone (CRZ). The establishment of the CRZ provided a wider platform to the Nepalese and Indian left-wing extremist organizations to strengthen their base of operations in the two countries.

The more radical groups in South Asia, including both the PWG and the Nepalese Maoists, are members of the 'Revolutionary Internationalist Movement' (RIM). In July 2001, about 10 extreme Left Wing (Maoist) groups in South Asia formed the Coordination Committee of Maoist Parties and Organization of South Asia (CCOMPOSA), in which the Nepalese Maoists, Maoist Communist Centre (MCC), PWG, Purbo Banglar Movement (Bangladesh), Communist Party of

Ceylon (Sri Lanka) and other Indian left-wing extremist parties became members.

The appearance of graffiti in remote villages in Naxalite strongholds, in Andhra Pradesh, upholding CCOMPOSA, indicates the spread of the idea of a common front of left-wing extremist groups in South Asia. The Central Committee of Maoists passed a resolution in January 2002 stating its intentions of working together with the PWG and the MCC in fighting the ban imposed on the latter two organisations in India, under the Prevention of Terrorism Act, 2002. In addition, latest reports indicate the setting up of an Indo-Nepal Border Region Committee consisting of the Maoists and the PWG to coordinate insurgent activities in North Bihar and along the border region.

For quite some time, the Maoists have also been working closely with the MCC for unification, consolidation and expansion of the Maoist movement in India and across South Asia. A careful examination of expansion of Naxalite activity in Bihar in the last two years would reveal the extent of support lent by the Nepali Maoists and an effort by the Nepalese insurgents to influence Maoist activities stretching across Andhra Pradesh, Chhattisgarh, Jharkhand, and Bihar.

The Bihar-Nepal border is easily permeable. Bihar has eight districts and 54 police stations situated on the border. In the recent past, the state police have arrested a number of Nepalese Maoists in the border districts of West and East Champaran, Sitamarhi, Sheohar and Madhubani. If reports are to be believed, the Nepalese have made full use of the general breakdown of law and order in the region to set up bases at several points along the border. Reports indicate the existence of training camps in the forests of Bagha in the West Champaran district. These forests and the accompanying harsh terrain makes it difficult to control insurgent activities in the area, which has emerged as a safe haven for the Nepalese insurgents.

The left-wing extremist group, the Communist Party of India—Marxist-Leninist (CPI-ML) Janashakthi, which has a marginal presence at least in six Indian States, but is very active in isolated and limited number of pockets in Andhra Pradesh, has expressed support to the Nepalese Maoists. It is a co-signatory, along with 41 other left-wing extremist groups ranging from South America to South East Asia, to a resolution that 'condemns and opposes the malpractice of the fascist state of Nepal' and demands 'life security' for imprisoned Maoist personnel, leaders and sympathisers.

The growing influence of Nepalese Maoists in other parts of India was unearthed after four of its personnel were arrested in West Bengal in February 2003. The arrested Maoists confessed during interrogation of their plan to use West Bengal as a corridor between their areas of domination in India and Nepal. Darjeeling and Siliguri would act as the important transit routes.

The Nepali residents in India, forming a strong population of nearly eight million, (particularly in Sikkim, Darjeeling, Siliguri, Shillong, Dehradun, Himachal Pradesh and Gorakpur-Lucknow belts) have established a countrywide organization called the Akhil Bharatiya Nepal Ekta Samaj (ABNES). The Government of India later banned the organization under the Prevention of Terrorism Act (POTA) in July 2002. ABNES was registered with the stated objective of securing unity among immigrant Nepalese residing in India and working for their welfare. However, it gradually became involved in subversive activities and began to function as a front for the Maoist insurgents of Nepal.

There is also some reportage about the Nepalese Maoists' links with insurgent groups active in India's Northeast like United Liberation Front of Assam (ULFA), Kamtapur Liberation Organisation (KLO), Gurkha National Liberation Front (GNLF) and Gurkha Liberation Organisation (GLO).

Though the exact nature of the relationship is so far unknown, the Maoists are also reported to have some links with the Liberation Tigers of Tamil Eelam (LTTE) in Sri Lanka. However, it is suspected that the Maoists have received arms training from LTTE operatives in the past and this practice may be continuing. Links between these two may have been facilitated through the PWG, which has a record of co-operation with the LTTE in arms procurement and training.

SALWA JUDUM

Salwa Judum is a word taken from the Gondi Adivasi

language. It means peace movement. The aim behind the movement is to create and maintain peace in the tribal areas by self-motivation of the adivasis. The movement started 15 years ago through the peaceful Peoples Awakening Programme and spread like wild fire. It can best be described as a spontaneous and self-initiated reaction of the natives of the area against the oppression of the naxalites. The overall objective of the movement is to form a village security committee. The main strength of the movement is that it stays away from all kinds of propaganda and publicity.

The movement has been hailed as a turning point in the fight against Naxalism. Thousands of villagers gather voluntarily and raise slogans against the Naxalites. They voice their willingness to make the supreme sacrifice to extricate the menace from their village. This is the first instance of its kind when the public openly raised their voices to oppose the Naxalites and expressed their desire to organize themselves to fight the problem.

Insights into the Reason behind 'Salwa Judum'

The economy of the area is predominantly rural with 85% of the population depending on agriculture and 82% living in villages. 46% of the total land area is covered by forests which include trees of Sal and Teak. Forestry and agriculture form the backbone of the economy. In addition, the state of Chatttisgarh can boast of rich deposits of Bauxite, Coal, Gold, Garnet, Quartz, Limestone, Diamonds and other minerals. Chattisgarh also has all the tin ore deposits in the country and is internationally reputed for providing one of the best quality of iron ore the world over. Unfortunately, these resources cannot be utilised to the optimum as industries and mining companies are reluctant to operate in the area due to the threat of the Naxalites. A few of the companies that are brave enough to venture in, end up paying protection money to the rebels.

Despite such generous endowments, the area finds itself in the grip of poverty and misery. This can be laid on the hands of the Naxalites who block developmental works and forbid the villagers to build roads or railway stations for their upliftment and security. In addition, they do not allow the villagers to pluck the Tendu leaves that are one of the main crops of the area. At places where Tendu farming is allowed, the Naxalites extract protection money or levy their own taxes on both the farm owners as well as the labourers who tend the crop.

The weekly markets are forced to remain shut for indefinite periods according to the whims of the Naxals. On the socio-religious front, the insulting of the tribal gods further infuriated the masses.

The setting up of the Special Task Force to counter the insurgency has taken the form of silver lining against the dark clouds that surround the lives of the villagers of the area. A number of hardcore Naxalies were killed and captured in police operations. With the inclusion of CRPF jawans and rumours of the arrival of additional Naga forces the villagers hoped that the balance of power would tilt in favour of the security forces and they were further encouraged to organise themselves against the exploitation and oppression committed by the Naxalites.

The Spread of Salwa Judum

The resolute public resistance unnerved the Naxalites and as a result the frustrated rebels formed a band of about 500 armed naxalites and militiamen carrying out attacks against villagers and security personnel. Within a year such bands targeted about 12 different villages. In one instance, Naxalites set fire to 300 huts of Salwa Judum activists showing no mercy even to women or children. A report has also been received of the burning of a one and a half year old infant to death.

Undeterred, the activists continued their peace marches and the movement gradually spread to Raipur, the capital of Chattisgarh, and also to some parts of Andhra Pradesh. Slowly but surely, the appeals of the Salwa Judum activists is having the desired effect. A steady stream of rebels are seen surrendering to authorities and security forces. Members of the Naxalites are willing to give up arms and be rehabillitaed in various government programmes.

The Salwa Judum movement has garnered support of public and political leaders from the area. Government forces and agencies take an active part in the campaign. The Chief Minister of the state and other leading ministers of the area have visited Salwa Judum camps and addressed the activists in a bid to show their support for the natives of the area.

The state government has taken strong steps to sustain and nurture the public resistance. Security has been beefed up to counter the escalation of violence. Village Defence Societies (VDS) have been formed under which the security forces impart security training to a few members of villages in Naxalite targeted areas. VDS members are appointed as Special Police Officers (SPO) and enjoy powers of police officers under the Police Act 1861. There are approximately 4000 SPO's in the area.

A number of health camps have been organised in addition to schools and hostels which have been opened in remote areas. Relief camps have been set up and accommodate around 43000 people.

Opposition to the Salwa Judum

Pandit Jawaharlal Nehru once said of the Indian communists, "The Indian communists are certainly not patriots. They are not interested in the well-being of Indian people, whatever other cause they may be seeking to serve. They speak about the country in a derogatory manner abroad. They preach violence which can only lead to a disastrous civil war."

Nehru's voice seems to be making itself heard once again with the leftist opposition to Salwa Judum and support to naxalite terrorists. Baffled by the opposition to the rebels, the leftist comrades are screaming shrill to stop the Judum on the grounds that it has led to a huge loss of lives and is only dividing the Vanvasi society, pitting one Vanvasi against the other.

The leftist logic implies that there should not have been any armed struggle for freedom in the pre-Independence era as fighting the much more powerful and well-armed British would have led to an even higher loss of lives. Through the past many decades the communists have supported the naxalites and their bid to establish a regime of the impoverished. But the Left perhaps turn a blind eye to the fact that the Naxalites often resort to violence as well, what with the cold-blooded killing of innocent civilians and brave security personnel, with their advanced weaponry procured from abroad out of foreign funds and the civilians' hard-earned money extorted through coercion.

Self-proclaimed "human rights activists" have denounced the Salwa Judum as an assault on the dignity of the Vanvasi population but remain silent on the atrocities committed by the naxalites on the very same Vanvasis.

The Naxalites make use of lofty and dignified words to prove the superiority of their ideology. They use terms like "human rights", "people's war", "democracy" to fool others into believing that they are well-intentioned and fighting for the larger good. Now, with the Salwa Judum gathering momentum, the rebels are faced with a true 'people's war', a practical implementation of 'human rights.' Ironically, the task of facing the true meaning of democracy is making them weak-kneed. The true strength of Salwa Judum can be garnered from the amount of opposition it has generated from the leftist quarters, left-leaning media, intellectuals, human rights groups, and social activists alike.

Salwa Judum is a native movement, a challenge thrown to those who have become puppets in the hands of outside powers for vested personal interests. It will go down in the history of mankind as a unique example of the power that is imbedded in every society but only few have the courage to explore and apply it.

CASE STUDIES

Orissa

Orissa has felt the nerves of naxal movement since 1968 when it was led by Nagbhushan Pattnaik there. But in the last twenty years or so the state has witnessed a strong naxalite movement. Earlier, it was Peoples' War Group (PWG) that was a dominant force in different parts with Maoist Communist Party (MCC) playing a lesser role in the progress of the movement. PWG was very influential in Gajapati, Ganjam, Koraput, Malkangiri, Nabarangapur and Rayagada districts. While, MCC's activities were restricted to Keonjhar, Mayurbhanj and Sundargarh districts of Orissa. But the formation of the Communist Party of India (Maoist) has proved to be big boost for naxalite movement in Orissa in particular and east India in general.

Now the Communist Party of India (Maoist) has spread the movement to different parts of Angul, Deogarh, Jajpur, Jharsuguda, Kandhmal and Sambalpur. CPI (M) has formed three zonal committees to carry its activities or what they call as their administrative functions. The three zonal committees are, Andhra-Orissa Border Special Zonal Committee (AOBSZC), Jharkhand-Bihar-Orissa Special Zonal Committee (JBOBSZC) and Dandakaranya Special Zonal Committee (DSZC). They are said to have some extremely dedicated cadre to look after their executive programmes.

Several reasons are responsible for growth and expansion of naxalism in Orissa but the singlemost reason is poverty. It is generally viewed that such a volatile phase of naxalism in Orissa is basically a product of the continuous process of underdevelopment. When other parts of India were developing the leaders and the harbingers of modern India overlooked Orissa, which has otherwise been rich in minerals, and other natural resources. The result has been obvious, the poverty at large scale in Orissa. According to the Planning Commission and Census reports Orissa is the poorest state in India, with about 48% of its population below poverty line. This means that approximately 17-28 million people in Orissa itself are officially living under BPL category. The area with larger population under BPL and the areas under greater influence of the naxalites corroborate each other.

It is not as if government has not tried to sort out the problem but the lacunae are that these efforts were not well directed, that is why all the government efforts have failed to produce the desired results. The Naxal strongholds of Rayagada, Koraput, Malkangiri, and Nabarangpur fall under the KBK region where a number of special programmes are in operation but poverty refuses to subside. A sum of Rs. 500 crores was released during 2003-04 and 2004-05 for KBK region as Special Central Assistance. Even the official documents suggest that a good amount of money has been spent in these regions. In spite of this the above-mentioned districts do figure among 150 of the most backward districts of India.

Similarly, Sundagarh and Keonjhar are among the poorest districts of India despite having very high concentration of mining resources and sponge iron units and despite having made significant contribution in the industrial development of the country. The region itself has in return got pollution and poverty. The state of development in such regions defies all logic of geography and economics. In such a situation naxal movement finds a very fertile ground, as dissatisfaction among the poor local populace is the commonest feeling here. The rise of mining and construction mafia has just added to the woes.

Orissa is one of those gifted landscape of the world, which is richly endowed with mines and minerals. Of the total mineral resources of India, Orissa has 99 per cent Chromate ore, 92 per cent of Nickel ore, 65 per cent of Graphite and Pyrophylite, 66 per cent of Bauxite, 31 per cent of Mineral sand, 32 per cent of Manganese, 28 per cent of Iron ore and 24 per cent of coal within its geographical boundary. Even then Orissa is the poorest state of the nation. Incidentally, the storehouse of the mineral resources in Orissa, that is, western and southern parts of the state are the most naxal-infested areas in the state.

The development strategy of the government with regard to Orissa has not been a success story by popular measure. Though, many small and big industries were established and irrigation projects were laid down, the local population is still among the poorest ones. And, the cruel reality of the ill thought out development strategy in resettlement operations owing to construction of mining, industry and irrigation project sites in Orissa resulted in the majority of inhabitants ending up with lower incomes, less land than before, less work opportunities, inferior housing, less access to the resources of the commons such as fuel-wood and fodder; and worse nutrition and physical and mental health.

Like everywhere else the Naxal movement has survived and sustained itself in Orissa because it revolves around the life of marginalized people of the state. The naxals have shown the poor people a dream of a society based on equality. Taking advantage of the acute poverty and rampant corruption in these remote corners of Orissa, the Naxals have shown them the dream of a revolution. On the other hand, the Orissa government has not come out with any concrete programme to deal with the Naxal menace. It is high time that the government realizes that the Naxals have come to represent a serious internal security problem.

Andhra Pradesh

Although the naxal movement originated in West Bengal,

Andhra Pradesh is the real naxal fortress and is the red cradle that has kept the movement alive and stood as the main base of naxalism in India. The Naxal movement started in Andhra Pradesh almost at the same time as in West Bengal but it was not a fertile ground for naxalites till as late as 1980. The movement started from the so-called 'Agency Area' in the forests of Srikakulam district. But it was only after the emergence of K Seetharamaiah and the formation of the People's War Group (PWG) in April 1980 that the state of Andhra Pradesh became the naxal hub of India. However, the merger of PWG and MCC in 2004 to form the Communist Party of India (Maoist) is seen as a significant development in the armed rebellion within the country. This merger marks a new phase in the naxal movement. Right now 19 of the 23 districts of Andhra Pradesh are under declared naxal infested areas. In these areas the organizational structure of the CPI (Maoist) includes six military platoons, 28 area committees, 66 local guerilla squads, and 16 action teams. There are three Special Zonal Committees in Andhra Pradesh. On the top of these administrative committees there is a governing body called the CPI (Maoist) State Committee.

Naxal movement since its inception has claimed 5-7 thousand lives in Andhra Pradesh alone. 2005 is considered as the bloodiest year in terms of casualties, as about 325 people died in the state due to naxal violence.

The government policies have also been responsible for the phenomenal growth of the naxalites in Andhra Pradesh. The election of 2004 was a proof of the politicians' interest in the power game instead of the plight of the people.

The governments in Andhra Pradesh have used naxalism as a poll plank. Every time the incumbent government starts things on positive note with the hope that naxal problem would be addressed adequately and that land reforms and other measures would be taken up to improve the situation and solve this continuously aggravating problem. But nothing is practically done on that front leaving the gentry dissatisfied. The successive governments have done just one thing that is to contain the naxal menace by means of force, and, this strategy has not proved to be a successful one.

Rajasekhar Reddy achieved power by harping on the slogans of economic development but he too has been using force only to counter the naxal problems. Such measures and attitute are not welocome in the present political and socio-economic scenario. His predecessor, Chandrababu Naidu was badly obsessed with the world bank's model of development and this resulted in large scale resentment among the peasants and rural and poor people. Everyone now knows that such policies were behind the large-scale suicides of farmers suffering from extreme distress. This has provided the Naxals with favourable conditions to consolidate and expand their movement.

As it has been said earlier, the naxal politics revolves around rural and land related issues. Hence, a streamlined strategy and a national agenda are immediately required to deal with the problem. Without any straw of doubt Land, Forest and Tribal development hold the key. Regrettably, Andhra Pradesh suffers from a dismal record of land reforms.

The chief minister of the state, Rajashekhar Reddy has recently formed a Land Commission. A separate department called 'Remote and Interior Area Development' has also been created. These are welcome beginnings and could become very effective provided the government carry them forward them till it regains the confidence of the poor and marginalized, because these measures attempt at dealing with the basic problems of naxalite movement at present. Under-development, poverty and unemployment have been the breeding ground for the naxal movement. So, if and when these genuine problems are addressed adequately the problems of naxalite movement would automatically start vanishing.

At least 460 persons have been killed in nine Naxalite-affected states during January-June 2006 according to the estimate of Asian Centre for Human Rights (ACHR). These include 90 security personnel, 189 alleged Naxalites and 181 civilians. Majority of the killings have been reported from Chhattisgarh (222), which accounted for 48.25% of the killings, followed by Andhra Pradesh (66), Jharkhand (62), Maharashtra (42), Bihar (36), Orissa (16), West Bengal (14), Madhya Pradesh (1) and Uttar Pradesh (1). Out of these 460 persons, 225 were killed during the second quarter (April to June) of 2006 with the highest number of killings being reported from Chhattisgarh (98), followed by Andhra Pradesh (45), Maharashtra (27) and Jharkhand (30). The security forces have killed 105 alleged Naxalites out of which 43 were killed in Andhra Pradesh, 32 in Chhattisgarh and 11 in Maharashtra. The claims of the security forces about the killing of the alleged Naxalites in encounters could not be verified. The Naxalites have also been responsible for the killing of 120 persons including 38 security forces, 75 civilians and 7 Naxalites in internecine conflict.

In his address to the Second Standing Committee Meeting of the Chief Ministers of the Naxalite affected States on 13 April 2006 Prime Minister Dr Manmohan Singh urged to take two-prong strategy: effective police response and socio-economic development of the Naxalite affected areas. A cursory scrutiny however shows that the governments' security measures outweigh development programmes needed to address the root causes of the Naxalism.

The issue has never been mere allocation of funds or launching of the special programmes. Article 245(1) of the Constitution of India provided for undertaking such programmes. However, the Planning Commission's evaluation of Integrated Tribal Development Project found misutilisation and divesion of funds meant for the lower strata of the society. Little corrective measures have been taken. Consequently, a large segments of the India's dispossessed and oppressed i.e. the Adivasis and the Dalits have remained untouched by any good governance in the last 58 years.

None of the special programmes announced by the States in 2006 address what Prime Minister called, "waiving debts by moneylenders, compounding of petty forest offences, coverage for every poor family in the affected districts under various schemes and better relief and rehabilitation to those displaced."

Rather, over 50,000 people have been displaced due to the Salwa Judum campaign in Chhattisgarh. The present trend of the rise in killings in the Naxal conflict would also not have reached such proportion had the State government of Chhattisgarh with tacit support from the Centre not sponsored the Salwa Jadum campaign. The Salwa Judum campaign has possibly more to do with the interests of many State political leaders than counter insurency operations.

As the governments undertake programmes either to move the civilians into the counter insurgency Salwa Judum camps or raise battalions from the populace of the Naxalites affected areas, the war has virtually come home. The Adivasis and the Dalits are increasingly getting sucked into India's civil war being waged under the leadership of the State and the Naxalites.

ACHR in its various reports and statements categorically held that the Adivasis and the Dalits who constitute substantial number of the populace in the Naxalite affected areas do not necessarily share the ideology of the Naxalites. But, it is the language of the Naxalites they can relate to because of their dispossession and deprivation; and their condemned situation provides the classical situation for the ultra-leftist uprising.

Addressing the Naxalite problem requires putting the interest of the Adivasis and Dalits on the highest priority. It cannot be addressed by more displacement, more bad governance, sub-human conditions and hunger inside the Salwa Judum camps manned by the State.

Socio-economic development of the Naxalite affected areas requires a seperate ministry for undertaking development programmes, coordination with various State governments and involvement of the civil society groups for ensuring the right to entitlement of the Adivasis and the Dalits. Unless this fact is appreciated, security centric policies will only intensify the conflict. It took over 50 years for the Centre to realise the need for a seperate ministry for development of the North East. The Central government can ignore the creation of a seperate ministry to undertake socio-economic development of the Naxalite affected areas only at its own perils.

STATE RESPONSE TO THE NAXAL PROBLEM

Naxalism is the single biggest internal security challenge ever faced by our country...the movement has gained in strength and has now spread to over 160 districts all over the country...the extremists are trying to establish 'liberation zones' in core areas where they are dispensing basic state functions of administration, policing and justice," Prime Minister Manmohan Singh noted in his address to the 2nd meeting of

Standing Committee of Chief Ministers on Naxalism on 13 April 2006. In the second meeting of the Standing Committee of Chief Ministers to chalk out strategies to counter Naxalism, Prime Minister suggested two-prong strategy of effective police response and socio-economic development of the Naxal-affected areas. The government proposed a joint unified command backed by a liberal surrender and rehabilitation policy.

The responses of the Central government and State governments are summarised below: Union Home Ministry and the common refrain The Central government set up a separate division in the Ministry of Home Affairs to tackle the Naxalite crisis. It has been supporting "Salwa Judum" type campaign and urged the States to take the experiences of Andhra police to train their police forces in the Naxalite affected areas.

The demand for more forces has been a common refrain. The Naxalite affected states want 100 central paramilitary battalions (with over 1 lakh ready-to-fight personnel) to go after the roughly 9,000 to 12,000 Naxalites. Eight states that have witnessed Naxalites' attacks presently have 29 such battalions. On 27 April 2006, the Centre sanctioned raising of 9 more India Reserve Battalions (IRB) comprising 9,000 police personnel for Naxalite-affected states of Andhra Pradesh, Jharkhand, Orissa, Karnataka, Uttaranchal, Uttar Pradesh and Haryana (one each) and two for worst-hit Chhattisgarh. It is also reportedly been considering sanctioning one India Reserve Battalion (IRB) each for Tamil Nadu and West Bengal. The Centre will spend around Rs. 20 crore on each battalion, which is higher than the earlier allocation of Rs. 13 crore.

The Union Home Ministry is considering to set up three or four specialised anti-Maoist centres at strategic locations - mainly at inter-state borders—each equipped with about five helicopters. The centres would be manned mainly by the Central Reserve Police Force (CRPF) and the pilots would be from the army or BSF. The MHA has also been considering to set up an elite commadno force exclusively dealing with the Naxalite insurgents.

In April 2006, Army Chief General JJ Singh suggested setting up an auxiliary force of ex-servicemen drawn from the Naxalite-affected States to carry out duties like detecting mines and explosive devices laid by Naxalites to attack the police and para-military forces.

Andhra Pradesh : Take the War Home I

In late March 2006, the State government of Andhra Pradesh issued orders to raise 15th Andhra Pradesh Special Police Battallion exclusively comprising of tribals from the Naxal affected areas. The battalion comprising of 1,000 personnel will have 10 Inspectors, 30 Sub-Inspectors, 45 Assistant Sub Inspectors, 277 Head Constables and 820 constables.

Bihar : Want the full Choppers

The Ministry of Home Affairs has allocated an annual budget of Rs. 23,000 crores for all the Naxalite affected States. Out of these, the state government of Bihar alone sought Rs. 21,000 crore to tackle the Naxal menace. That leaves the Central government with Rs. 2,000 crore for the rest of the states. Bihar was asked to trim up the proposal.

Chhattisgarh : Demand Choppers

The Chhattisgarh State Government demanded choppers for reconnaissance and para dropping of the forces in the Maoist strongholds. With a view to recruit more eligible people, read as Adivasis, to strengthen the State Police, the Chhattisgarh Government on 28 April 2006 relaxed parameters of recruitment by reducing the required height of 158 cm to 153 cm for the candidates. Jharkhand: Price for the soldiers' limbs 'If any of the 25,000 personnel engaged in anti-Naxal drive suffers fatal wounds or permanent total disability or loses two limbs or sight, his or her family will be entitled to a maximum benefit of Rs. 11.5 lakh," stated Jhakhand's Home Minister Sudesh Mahto.

In April 2006, the Jharkhand government increased the insurance to dependants of jawans killed in operations against Naxalites in the state to Rs. 21.5 lakh, instead of Rs. 10 lakh which are being paid presently. The annual premium amount of Rs. 2,47,50,000 for 2006 has already been paid by the state government for the "group personal accident insurance policy". About 25,000 security personnel engaged in anti-insurgency operations including from other states will also be benefited. The insurance amount would be apart from the Rs. 10 lakh package, awarded by the State Government to families of such martyrs.

On 20 April 2006, the Jharkhand government also announced a new surrender policy. It offered Rs. 50,000 in cash to each surrendered Naxalite and a monthly allowance of Rs. 2,000. Other benefits include cash equivalent to the price of the weapon surrendered, a life insurance cover worth Rs. 10 lakhs, vocational training for two years, one acre of agricultural land, health and educational facility for their children. The Naxalites will also be entitled to a lawyer to fight their case in the court.

In case, the surrendered Naxalites want different lawyer, the government would bear all the expenses. The village, whose residents help in mass surrender of Naxalites, will get Rs. 25 lakhs as bonus for development and the villagers would decide how to use the money for the development of their area.

Karnataka : Secret Plans

"I will not publicise it. It will be revealed after the problem is tackled",—declared Chief Minister Mr Kumaraswamy on his secret plan to tackle the Naxalite problem.

Earlier, the state government decided to allocate special funds for developing Naxal-affected villages in Karnataka over the next two years. Each gram panchayat, village council, would be given Rs. 10 lakh a year for two years for developing Naxal affected villages in their jurisdiction. As many as 315 villages under 152 gram panchayats in 11 districts have been identified as Naxal-affected. The state government has directed the gram panchatyats to prepare a comprehensive development plan as per the guidelines of the Kugrama Suvarna Scheme by 15 May 2006. The gram panchayats will be the implementing agencies for these programmes. The government has also directed use of other grants from the government, zilla and taluk panchayats for developing these villages on priority.

Orissa : Extension of the Ban

On 9 June 2006, Orissa government banned CPI (Maoists) and seven of its front organizations—Damana ratirodh Manch,

Revolutionary Democratic Front, Chasi Mulia Samiti, Kui Lawenga Sangha, Jana Natya Mandali, Krantikari Kisan Samiti and Bal Sangam.

The Orissa government has also approved a comprehensive rehabilitation package for the Naxals who surrender. The rehabilitation package consists of payment up to Rs. 10,000 on acceptance of surrender, payment up to Rs. 20,000 for surrendering arms and ammunition, allotment of homestead land, house building grant up to Rs. 25,000, Rs. 15,000 for marriage, assistance to take loan up to Rs. 2 lakhs from banks on which there will be no interest for two years, subsidy up to Rs. 50,000 after repayment of 75 per cent of the loan, free medical treatment in government hospitals within the state and cost of fees and textbooks for study up to high school. The government also proposed to withdraw cases involving minor offences against surrendered Naxalites.

Uttar Pradesh : Take the war home II

In late June 2006, Uttar Pradesh government declared to raise a special battalion of the Provincial Armed Constabulary, comprising local youth of the Naxalite-affected districts of Sonebhadra, Chandauli and Mirzapur to tackle the Naxalite problem in Uttar Pradesh.

West Bengal

Addressing 28 years of neglect On 23 June 2006, West Bengal government announced Rs. 50-crore special allocation for underdeveloped rural areas of the state, most of which are Maoist strongholds to intensify development efforts centering on production, employment, education, training, public health and housing in these areas. In addition, Rs. 5 crore has been specially earmarked for Paschimanchal (western zone), which comprises 74 blocks of Bankura, Purulia, West Midnapore, Burdwan and Birbhum districts. A separate department for Paschimanchal development has been created to expedite the implementation of poverty alleviation programmes. But the department has no budget of its own.

The government has also proposed to take loans worth Rs. 150 crore from the National Bank for Agricultural and Rural

Development (NABARD) for the development of the three regions—Paschimanchal, the Sunderbans and north Bengal. But funds often do not reach the tribal people in the impoverished region.

SOLUTION : FOLLOW THE PM'S PRESCRIPTIONS

Union Home Ministry is scheduled to convene a high level meeting of the Chief Secretaries and Director Generals of Police of the Naxalite affected States in Bhuvaneshwar on 21 July 2006 to take stock of the situations. The meeting to be chaired by Union Home Secretary V K Duggal will obviously focus on security measures.

While the state has the right, prerogative, and duty to take necessary security measures, Asian Centre for Human Rights firmly believes that the policies of the government must address the root causes of the Naxalite problem as lucidly articulated by none other than the Prime Minister of India in his address to the Second Standing Committee Meeting of the Chief Ministers of the Naxalite affected States on 13 April 2006. Prime Minister Dr. Manmohan Singh stated that "exploitation, artificially depressed wages, iniquitous socio-political circumstances, inadequate employment opportunities, lack of access to resources, under developed agriculture, geographical isolation, lack of land reforms, all contribute significantly to the growth of the Naxalite movement."

There is no military solution to the Naxalite crisis and many State governments have suddenly woken up to the abject neglect that allowed the Naxals to strengthen their support base and have announced specialprogrammes. As stated earlier, there has not been any dearth of such programmesbut these programmes seldom reached to those who need it most. In many areas including those vacated because of the Salwa Judum campaign, the edifice of the State structure does not exist. The challenge for the government is to establish the machanisms to make such programmes effective with full respect for human rights and fundamental freedoms, and without causing any further alienation.

GOVERNMENT OF INDIA

The Ministry of Home Affairs (MHA) is the nodal ministry on 'law and order' at the Government of India. The ministry was once in charge of the development and protection of the scheduled castes and tribes (SCs and STs), a special Constitutional responsibility entrusted to the Government of India. This implied a strong social justice component to its activities. The subject has now been transferred to the Ministry of Social Justice and Welfare (MSJ&W).

With its social justice component in law and order work, the MHA looked seriously at the problem of 'atrocities' against the SC's and the ST's by the upper castes and classes often with the support and connivance of the police while examining the 'Naxalite' violence which attracts considerable dalit/adivasis support. The Civil Rights Cell in the ministry monitored and reported on the increasing 'atrocities' against the dalits and adivasis. The Parliament took interest in the policies and programs for the development and protection of the SC's and ST's. The ministry had to reply to Parliament questions (often trying to provide as little information as possible to that august body!) In view of its police power, clout and resources, the MHA was in a position to persuade state governments to take pro-active social justice, development and protective measures for these historically exploited communities. The transfer of the subject to the newly-created Ministry of Social Justice and Empowerment (MSJE), which lacks the prestige and resources of the MHA has been unfortunate as it lacks the ability to take care of the special constitutional responsibility for the dalits and adivasis. The absence of the MSJE from the CMs conference on Naxalite/Maoist violence was strange. Representatives of the two National Commissions on the SC's and the ST's as well as the ministers and officials of state governments dealing with the development and protection of SC/ST's were also absent.

This context must be borne in mind while considering the deliberations at the conference of state chief ministers held in 2006 to debate the growing Naxalite/Maoist violence. The conference took a largely law and order view of the problem. Branding the problem a major 'national security challenge', it ignored the social justice component in the development and protection of the dalits and adivasis. The SC/ST's together constitute about a quarter of the Indian population; they are largely poor, uneducated and uncared for and are often made victims of development. They constitute a significant support base for the Naxalite/Maoist movement.

As the nodal ministry on law and order, MHA has the responsibility of preparing national policy framework on conflict management and issue guidelines to state governments. The huge numbers of Central Paramilitary Forces (CPFs) recruited by the MHA for specific purposes, are frequently used for local conflict management in the states in clear departure from the intentions of the founding fathers of the Constitution. A former Home Secretary, however, referring to this conundrum, described India as a 'dual polity' (Srinivasavaradan, 1992).

The MHA, despite its manifold responsibilities, is devoid of a meaningful information base on conflict situations across the country. Its information base consists mainly of police reports from the IB and the state governments. To rectify the information deficiency in the ministry, a former Home Secretary set up the Research and Policy (R&P) Division (1967). The Division submitted a seminal report on the "Causes and Nature of Agrarian Tensions". Similar reports followed on several patterns of violence in the country. However, it became a victim of an internal power struggle and was eventually wound up. The information gap in the ministry persists with disastrous consequences. Civil servants being 'philosophers of the short term' have relied on the deployment of the Central Paramilitary Forces (CPF's).

The paper is in five parts: i) the current strategy and tactics of the MHA in dealing with the Naxalite/Maoist movement; ii) the information crisis in the MHA; iii) the Naxalite/Maoist movement today; iv) alternative policy framework for tackling the Naxalite movement; and v) structural reforms of the Union Home Ministry, the IB and the state and central police forces to meet the rising aspirations of the people keeping in view the Preamble, Directive Principles of State Policy and Fundamental Rights of the Constitution of India.

CURRENT STRATEGY AND TACTICS OF THE MHA

The Prime Minister in his March 14, 2006 address to the standing committee of chief ministers of states affected by Naxalite/Maoist violence had said that this violence was the biggest national security threat. The Union Home Minister in his statement in the Lok Sabha on March 1, 2006 revealed that 26 CPF battalions would be given to the states to deal with Naxalite/Maoist violence. On March 13, 2006, the minister asked the states not to enter into dialogue with the CPI (Maoists) unless they gave up arms. He told the meeting of the standing committee of chief ministers that 'local resistance' such as 'Salwa Judum' in Chhattisgarh will be 'up-scaled' (Navlakha, 2006).

The situation in the Dantewara district (population: 0.8 million) of the largely tribal state of Chhattisgarh had assumed special importance in view of the violence of the 'Salwa Judum' activists backed by the central paramilitary forces and the violence of the Maoists well entrenched in the district (Balagopal, 2006; Navlakha, 2006; PUCL, 2006). A group of distinguished citizens after a visit to the district in 2006 reported that the victims of violence from both sides were the innocent tribal people who were not in any way part of the conflict. A closely argued analysis of the violence by both sides brought out the need for a 'political handling of the issue and not suppression by brute force' as is being attempted by the central and state governments (Balagopal, 2006).

The National Common Minimum Program (NCMP) of the United Progressive Alliance (UPA) government (2004), which said that "the UPA government is concerned about the growth of extremist violence and other forms of terrorist activity in different states. This is not merely a law and order problem but a deeper socio-economic issue which will be addressed more meaningfully than has been the case so far. Fake encounters will not be permitted".

At the DGP's/IGP's conference, 2005 held in New Delhi, the Coordination Centre of police officers circulated a document titled "Leftwing Extremism-Emerging Dimensions" stating the threat perception on the part of the IB and the police leadership of the concerned states. There was a huge gap in the information provided in the police report and the one that emanated from the citizens group regarding the nature and causes of the violence in Chhattisgarh. However, relying on police reports and disregarding the commitments made in NCMP, the MHA geared up as never before, to deploy the Central Paramilitary Forces on a massive scale in order to crush the Naxalite/Maoist mobilization going on in several states.

The annual report of the MHA for 2005-06 did refer to the statement made in the NCMP though it noted with deep concern the rapid spread of the Naxalite violence in several states. The report mentioned the Naxalite/Maoist issue as the third major 'national security issue' after the situation in Jammu & Kashmir (J&K) and in the north-eastern region. The following table reports some facts relating to the violence during 2002-5.

Head	*2002*	*2003*	*2004*	*2005*
No. of Incidents	1,465	1,597	1,533	1,594
No. of Civilians Killed	382	410	466	516
No. of Policemen Killed	100	105	100	153
No. of Naxalites Killed	141	216	87	223

Source : (GOI, 2006, p. 23).

The MHA report added that in 2005, while the number of incidents had gone up by 4 percent over those of 2004, the 'civilian' casualties have gone up by 11 percent and of police personnel killed by 53 percent. It stated that 76 districts in the nine States of Andhra Pradesh, Bihar, Chhattisgarh, Jharkhand, Orissa, Maharashtra, Madhya Pradesh, Uttar Pradesh and West Bengal are badly affected. The level of violence was significant in Andhra Pradesh, Chhattisgarh, Jharkhand, Bihar, Maharashtra and Orissa.

In 2005, violence was reported from 509 police stations in 11 states out of a total of 12476 in the country including the above states. The State-wise breakup incidents and deaths for the years 2002 and 2005 were given. The annual report stated that the trends in violence included militarization and consolidation, attacks on police personnel, attacks on government/private property, holding of people's courts and forging of linkages with the Maoists of Nepal.

The MHA adopted a multi-pronged strategy to contain the violence including building up of 'local capabilities' to improve intelligence gathering; strengthening of the administrative machinery to redress grievances; improving delivery of accelerated socio-economic development; promoting employment opportunities; encouraging 'local resistance'; and encouraging affected State governments to promote peace initiatives.

Further, three schemes were administered to strengthen the security apparatus at the State level: reimbursement of Security-Related Expenditure (SRE) with release of substantial funds in advance (Rs 2000 Crores in 2005-06), police modernization and up-gradation in terms of modern weaponry, mobility, and communication infrastructure; and finally, funds to raise India Reserve (IR) battalions to augment State police forces. Inter-State Intelligence Support Teams (ISISTS) were being set up in the States to strengthen intelligence collection and sharing in addition to sharing of intelligence by Central agencies with State agencies; special efforts to step up training of police forces; and increased vigil along the Indo-Nepal border.

On the development front, the MHA has advised State governments to ensure integrated development of the affected districts. Under the Backward Districts Initiative (BDI), Rs. 2475 Crores have been sanctioned by the Central government for 55 Naxal-affected districts. The ministry of environment and forests has issued general approval for the use of up to 1 hectare of forest land for security and socio-economic infrastructure in forest areas. Stepping up of implementation of Panchayats (Extension to Scheduled Areas) Act 1996, strengthening of administrative machinery by the posting of competent and willing officers to Naxalite areas, encouraging 'local resistance groups', 'public perception management', organization of tribal youths' cultural exchange programs are the other development initiatives.

Finally, review mechanisms at the central level included a Task Force on Naxalism/Maoism under a Special Secretary of the MHA with a nodal officers from affected states and others; a Coordination Centre headed by the Union Home Secretary and consisting of State Chief Secretaries and Directors General of Police and others; and a standing committee of Chief

Ministers and others under the chairmanship of the Union Home Minister.

The MHA's approach made a reference to socio-economic issues but did not address the land question, the rural development strategy, the increasing violence against the SCs and STs or the massive displacement of these communities as a result of development projects and so on. It mentioned 'project implementation in the rural areas'. As in the past, such efforts continue to be sabotaged by a corrupt administrative structure at the cutting edge level, in collusion with the rural power structure. Thus, the envisaged measures did not, in practice, constitute a sharp break from the traditional law and order approach. The existing administrative structure obstructs effective rural development because of its caste-class linkages with the existing rural power structure and it needs to be addressed. Further, the inherited administrative structure is basically regulatory given the colonial regime's preoccupation with law and order. The post-independence development administrative machinery is a superimposition on the inherited regulatory structure led by the District Magistrate (DM).

Furthermore, the increasing numbers of the state armed police and central paramilitary forces for public order management is in strong contrast to the rather tenuous framework for development administration and social justice.

INFORMATION CRISIS IN THE MHA

One of the ironies of the functioning of the MHA is that it was aware of the deficiencies in its information system and conflict analysis. It set up the Research and Policy(R&P) Division in 1967. However, it took no steps to set up institutional mechanisms to utilize the findings of the Division for policy making. It continued to rely on the British precedent of using force to tackle violence. A distinguished former Home Secretary (Srinivasavaradan, 1992) said that the available expertise at the bureaucratic level to understand, anticipate and evaluate an intricate problem was inadequate and amateurish. The situation in some cases was salvaged in the past because of the flexibility of the system, the sagacity of the political leadership and its openness to information from all quarters.

Responsiveness to public opinion of all shades is important. Awareness and sensitivity contributes to responsiveness but it can never be provided by official briefings alone. The variety and persistence of the problems the polity faces calls for the creation of inter-disciplinary study-cum-action groups to monitor and analyze socio-economic trends. This was never done.

Srinivasavaradan further noted that the Naxalite movement, which started in tribal areas, took roots in tracts where exploitation of the weaker sections was chronic, blatant and unmitigated. The political response of the MHA initially was sound as it was based on the perception that the objective socio-economic conditions, which were breeding and sustaining the violence must be dealt with. However, when the intensity of the violence abated and it became endemic and sporadic, the political response took the shape of the standard administrative action of deploying the central paramilitary forces in the affected areas. Allegations of fake encounters, illegal arrests and other misdeeds tended to be swept under the carpet. Srinivasavaradan concluded that 'in dealing with problems of societal transition, excessive preoccupation with peace and order, ignoring issues of law and justice, can prove expensive in the long run'. Lack of steadfastness of purpose is not desirable in dealing with basic nation building tasks though reasonable success was seen in fire-fighting operations during war, drought and scarcity.

When issues with long term implications came up, the traditional responses and mechanisms of the MHA were found deficient. The prevailing ad-hocism and amateurishness could only be remedied by additional inputs of knowledge, skill and vision through multidisciplinary research and policy analysis. The setting up of the Research and Policy (R&P) Division of the MHA largely coincided with the emergence of the Naxalite movement in the late 1960s. But the studies done R & P Division were hardly ever utilized in policy making for want of appropriate mechanisms.

The administrative obstacles to the implementation of agrarian reforms such as the lack of qualifications and integrity necessary for the administration of tenancy reforms on the part of civil servants who were overburdened with other responsibilities; insufficient coordination between the state agency for land reforms and the agriculture and cooperative departments; lack of correct and updated land records; weak budgetary support; illiteracy and ignorance on the part of tenants; dual role of landlords as money lenders; heterogeneous interests of the village population; and the gulf in social status separating tenants from landlords, influenced the administrative and judicial authorities handling land disputes. The administrative, police and judicial structures of post-colonial India given their colonial origins function mainly on the basis of past precedents. Besides, law and order and rural development were both state subjects under the Constitution. The MHA was unable to emphasize the importance of ameliorative social action to state governments affected by Naxalite activities and to deal with the socio-economic issues highlighted by the movement separately from the issue of violence. However, the immediate issue became one of law and order and the socio-economic context was brushed under the carpet by states.

In the early 1980's, following a series of incidents of violence in the Jehanabad district of Bihar, involving the death of a large number of the rural poor, Prime Minister Indira Gandhi, who was sensitive to social change ordered the setting up of a Central Team to go to Bihar for a first hand study. The Team was led by Dr. Manmohan Singh, then Member-Secretary Planning Commission and included the author. On arrival in Bihar the Team found a district administration proud of its record of successfully maintaining public order though at the cost of a number of innocent lives. District officials took some time to realize that the purpose of the Team's visit was not to appreciate the good work done on the law and order front but to evaluate the implementation of policies to enforce minimum wages, social dignity and rural development programmes. The state police reported the number of deaths in police action to be 12 persons, all of them naxalites. The in its report to the MHA had repeated the same figure. The figure was well below the number emerging from press reports. At a subsequent meeting in the MHA, the state chief secretary admitted that the number of those killed in police action was nearer 60 persons none of whom was a 'Naxalite'.

In another major incident of Naxalite violence in the Dharmapuri district of Tamil Nadu in the early 1980's, it was found that most of those killed in police encounters were innocent persons whose crime had been to demand minimum wages, social dignity and civil rights. The police officer in charge of the district when, confronted with this, maintained that 'naxalites' did not believe in the Constitution of India and therefore the state police were not bound by strictly constitutional methods in dealing with them.

Studies in two districts of Bihar and Tamil Nadu revealed a very different picture from that portrayed in intelligence reports sent to the ministry. The studies confirmed scholarly findings that social movements of the rural poor originated by articulating demands, which correspond to the most concretely, felt grievances and needs. When the elite/state machinery, instead of responding positively to the demands, tries to block the growing movement, it becomes more radical; and even revolutionary, with attempts at violent suppression. When the just and legitimate demands are violently suppressed, the State tends to lose its legitimacy.

The main demands of the rural poor related to the issues of land, wages and social oppression. A large number of them are landless agricultural workers. And a landless person in rural India is a non-person. Any attempt at getting possession of land, security of tenure, payment of minimum wages is seen as an attempt of disturb the social status quo and as soon as this happens public order and tranquility are threatened and all the relevant provisions of the IPC and the CrPC can be invoked by the rural elite and the state machinery to preserve the status quo.

A significant line of enquiry from the administrative point of view would be to look at the systematic patterns of power and domination that arise in rural society and the injustice and exploitation that are associated with the unequal distribution of land and other productive assets. Further, the patterns of interaction between the administration at the local level and the rural power structure in the context of subsistence agriculture in most part of rural India also needed to be looked at.

Unfortunately, a power struggle that ensued over providing reliable information to the government witnessed the rapid decline of the R&P Division. The social science insights, essential for a proper understanding of the causes and nature agrarian tensions in the country during the 1980s were not forthcoming. The reports submitted by the IB were far from adequate. The crisis was aggravated by the non-institutionalization of adequate policy instruments to utilize academic studies in policy making.

NAXALITE/MAOIST MOVEMENT TODAY

Compared to the Naxalbari movement of the earlier phase, the (CPI Maoist)-led armed struggle is seen by observers to be at a more advanced level. It has spread over a larger area and has survived for over two decades. The strongest guerilla zone remains the Dandakaranya forest region in central India covering eleven districts across the four states of Andhra Pradesh, Maharashtra, Chhattisgarh and Madhya Pradesh. The Maoist Communist Centre (MCC) of Bihar and Jharkhand claims that its influence in the region extends to a population of about 12 million people of tribal origin. Even though more widespread than the earlier Naxalite movement, the Maoists of today have not yet been able to build powerful country wide political movements. The overall picture is one of a relatively strong militant outfit with popular support in its strongholds in the south, central and eastern regions. Outside its core areas, the Indian state has been able to prevent Maoist entry into the national political arena.

TOWARDS AN ALTERNATIVE STRATEGY

During the 1980s, the MHA was not just a law and order ministry but was responsible for the important subject of the development of the Scheduled Castes (SCs) and Scheduled Tribes (STs). Initiatives such as Special Component Plan for the former and the Tribal Sub- Plan for the latter were started and implemented on the ground through the state governments. The ministry also took a keen interest in the increasing violence against the SCs and STs in the country and initiated effective measures to stop the violence and to punish the offenders with 'deterrent rapidity'. The Civil Rights Cell monitored the trends of violence and prepared reports for the Cabinet and Parliament. The MHA was a strong and powerful ministry with funds and police forces to compel the state governments to follow the central guidelines and instructions on issues of violence, development and social justice.

The creation in the subsequent period of the Ministry of Social Justice and Empowerment and the allocation of the subject of the development of Scheduled Castes and Tribes to that ministry along with the issue of socio-political violence against these communities reduced the MHA to a purely law and order apparatus. As a consequence, the annual report of the ministry for the year 2005-06 reads like a strange document devoted entirely to Naxalite violence with nothing to say on the increasing number and intensity of violence against the SCs and STs in the recent period. Such a juxtaposition of the naxalite violence with the increasing violence against the SC's and ST's is necessary for appreciation of both 'violence of development' and 'development of violence' and to devise appropriate measures in coordination with the state governments. In this sense, the creation of a separate Ministry of Social Justice and Empowerment was not perhaps an altogether happy development for the Scheduled Castes and Tribes.

The process of commercialization of forest resources has reduced the access of indigenous communities to these resources. Alienation of tribal land to richer non-tribal elements from outside is a significant factor in tribal unrest. Displacement due to the construction of large dams and other industries has impoverishment of these communities, strengthening demands for tribal self governance.

Government programs for tribal development have had adverse consequences for tribal communities as documented in several studies including those conducted on behalf of the government of India (GOI, 2008). The extension of Panchayati Raj Institutions (PRI's) to tribal areas can become an instrument of empowerment only after steps are taken to restore indigenous rights over land and forest. The setting up of the new states of Chhattisgarh, Jharkhand and Uttaranchal to enable tribal participation in governance and decision making at decentralized levels, is largely ineffective due to the unchanged character and mindset of the administrative and police set-up.

B. Mungekar, Member Planning Commission of India is reported to have prepared a report (Navlakha, 2006) showing that between 1951 and 1990, 40 million people were displaced as result of development projects. Of these 40 percent were tribal people. Only 25 percent of the displaced have so far been 'rehabilitated'. The adequacy and quality of 'rehabilitation' has come into serious question especially in the context of the recent controversy over the Sardar Sarovar Project (Roy 2006). In the light of this, it is not surprising that the naxalite movement has found support among those sections of Scheduled Tribes who became victims rather than beneficiaries of development.

The issue was examined in depth by Dr. B. D. Sharma, then Commissioner for Scheduled Castes and Tribes in his 28th Report to the President of India (Sharma, 2000). The report elaborated a Constitutional schema for establishing an egalitarian society with clear provisions for countering simultaneously the inequities of tradition and the 'backlash of modernization' in the nation's development. The focus was on the dalits and the adivasis. The assessment was that the outcome of the developmental measures taken plus the adverse forces already at work was a negative one as indicated by the accentuation of deprivation and the 'relentless slide back' in the fortunes of these communities notwithstanding some token achievements such as 'reservations' in government jobs. The analysis laid bare the 'omissions, distortions, subterfuges and the studied silence on vital issues' in order to protect vested interests. The people were paying a heavy price for the so-called 'development'. All the institutions of the state, executive, legislative and judicial, had abdicated their constitutional responsibility of safeguarding the interest of the deprived sections. The executive in particular, with its distorted role perception, is working against the interests of those whose wellbeing is its sacred trust. The action taken on the report by the government amounted to undermining constitutional values and trivialization of institutions by those who had the responsibility to protect them.

However, the model that was adopted in practice legitimized divestiture of the indigenous people's traditionally recognized rights in the name of 'development'. Not merely were the immemorial customary rights of the tribals ruthlessly violated but they were made to appear as trespassers in their own lands. All this was being done in spite of the concern expressed in the Constitution's Fifth Schedule that the laws of the land should be suitably adapted in their application to Scheduled areas, a responsibility entrusted to the executive as part of its duty for the advancement of the Scheduled Tribes. To accomplish this task, the executive was conferred with special powers. The deliberate non-use of these powers resulted in not just unconstitutional and unjust governance but also in cruel and callous administration.

In the light of this analysis, the Report to the President also examined the issue of self governance at the village level and the disastrous effect of the non-recognition of command over community resources, which had resulted everywhere in disorganization, displacement and destitution of the adivasis. There could be no peace in the Scheduled Areas so long as the confrontation between the people and the state continued on the issue of self governance, particularly on the intimately associated question of the command over resources.

A recent paper by Amit Bhaduri and Medha Patkar published in EPW (January 3 2009) meaningfully carries forward the discussion started by BD Sharma.

The current strategy of the MHA, as spelt out in its annual reports for 2004-5 and 2005-6, appear retrograde and counterproductive in the light of this analysis. The deployment of paramilitary forces on a large scale in the interior tribal areas of the country does not solve the problem but can cause immense misery to the common people. The whole policy of raising and deploying central paramilitary forces for local conflict management is based on faulty thinking and leads to serious internal security disasters. Paramilitary units as India Reserve battalions, which the Centre is encouraging states to raise to deal with internal security problems cannot be effective since their basic military type of training involves no local contact or interaction or understanding of the local population and problems. A recent visit to Chhattisgarh, where a Nagaland based IR battalion has been deployed, indicated emerging tensions between the district police leadership and the Naga battalion leadership since the latter is prioritized over the former, which is basically responsible for law and order management. A similar tension had emerged in Punjab earlier when the National Security Guard (NSG) was deployed over the head of the state DG of Police who was basically responsible for law and order in the state.

Similarly, it has been found in the northeast that lack of local knowledge on the part of the central paramilitary forces (CPFs) often led to disasters for the men, who were ambushed because they followed misleading intelligence provided to them by some interested local elements. Further, the induction of CPF's often leads to tensions between them and the local police responsible for law and order and to demoralization of central of the central forces.

REFORMS IN THE MHA AND THE POLICE

The discussion above indicates the need for far-reaching reforms of the MHA and the rest of the central and state political systems in India as indicated by me in a separate study (Subramanian, 2007). Police reforms in India have been much under discussion recently with little or no action. The Soli Sorabji report on the Model Police Act 2006 has been accompanied by the seven directions of the Supreme Court of India (CHRI, 2009) relating to : (i) the setting up of State Security Commissions; (ii) tenure and selection of the state DGP; (iii) tenure of other state police officials; (iv) Police Complaints Authorities; (v) Police Establishment Boards; (vi) separation of investigation from law and order; (vii) National Security Commission, Acceptance of the Sorabji report and the implementation of the Supreme court directions have been met with dilatory responses. There has been no attempt by the central government to solicit the views of the civil society.

Police reforms would have to address the following key issues.

- The paramilitary structures of even the civilian police which have led to most of its regressive political-organizational features (Arnold, 1986; Baxi, 1982 Subramanian, 2007);
- While the Supreme Court in its seven directions has rightly focused on curbing 'political interference' in

police work, it must be remembered that sometimes 'political intercession' with the police by a non-power holding politician on behalf of his constituents to set right a police wrong or to register a complaint may be 'democratic' in a society like ours with an authoritarian police structure and its oppressive behavior with the public. At other times, the management failures of the police leadership in giving relief to the people may lead to such 'political intercession' at the local level. 'Politicization of the police is the price we have to pay for the democratic functioning of our polity' (Verma, 2005). This type of political intervention is to be distinguished from the frequent and highly objectionable 'political interference' by the politician holding executive power who directs the police to do as he wills, against the Constitution and the law.

- The role of police intelligence agencies at the centre and in the states, which are the main sources of information on social conflicts in the government; reports by policemen, who are not trained in social analysis, carry a pervasive bias against social movements which assert the legal, social and human rights of poor people and a bias in favor of 'security of the state'. Policemen often consider such movements for social justice as 'incipient insurgencies'. Other publicly available reports produced by scholars and activists bring out the real socio-economic basis of such movements and contradict police reports. However, governments have a tendency to rely on police reports in such cases and go ahead to provide the police with increased fire power, mobility and manpower contrary to the need to undertake a political dialogue with the disaffected public; the notorious case of Binayak Sen is a good example of misuse of police intelligence against human rights activists; the situation points to the need for serious reform of the information systems in government;
- The recasting of the Police Act 1861 must be accompanied by concomitant changes in the Indian Penal Code (IPC), 1860, and the Criminal Procedure

Code, 1861 which, given their colonial origins, prioritize state security issues such as 'Offences Against the State', 'maintenance of public order and tranquility', political intelligence collection, to the neglect of human security issues (Gupta, 1974);

The need for decentralization of the highly centralized police structure, which was suitable for the British Raj but is not relevant in a rapidly decentralizing governance system of a democratic country, involving the three tier system of Panchayati Raj Institutions (PRIs), operating from the district level to the village. The PRIs are constitutionally mandated to undertake crucial developmental functions but their work is hamstrung by the non-provision of adequate 'functions, functionaries and finances' (Bandyopadhyay, 2007); there is a need to decentralize the police structures in a way as to align them with the PRIs and make the police functionaries at the district level and below accountable to the heads of the PRIs; 'democracy at the top and bureaucracy at the bottom' as exists today must be abolished;

- There is need to reconsider the role of about a million strong central paramilitary forces.
- The need to review and revise from a human rights point of view, the Police Regulations, Police Manuals and Standing Orders in different states, which provide practical guidelines for day to day police activity at the state, district and police Station levels;
- Police corruption is a serious but still understudied issue.
- A recent study on police torture (People's Watch, 2008) states that up to 1.8 million people in India are being tortured in police custody every year. Another study has delved into police ill-treatment of minorities, dalits, adivasis, and women (Subramanian, 2007). This needs to be tackled.
- The culture of secrecy and non-transparency that pervades police organizations.
- Discontinuance of repressive legislations, such as POTA, CLAA and AFPSA, in dealing with political

movements, which are better dealt with by political means and political dialogues in a 'deliberative democracy' rather than by police repression (Planning commission, 2008; Kannabiran, 2008).

8

Conclusion

HOW TO TACKLE MAOISTS

The continuing inability of the government—whether at the Centre or in the States—to counter effectively the spread of the activities of the Maoist insurgents-cum-terrorists was once again demonstrated by the temporary control established by the CPI-Maoist and its front organisation called the People's Committee Against Police Atrocities in 17 villages spread across some 300 square kilometres in the Lalgarh area in West Bengal.

The People's Committee, with the backing or at the instigation of the Maoists exploited local anger over alleged police excesses against the tribals following an alleged Maoist attempt to kill Chief Minister Buddhadeb Bhattacharjee through a landmine blast in November 2008.

What started as a protest movement against police excesses was transformed by the Maoists into a violent political movement. The hesitation of the governments of West Bengal and India to act strongly against the Maoist-instigated committee at the very beginning was apparently due to electoral considerations arising from the recently-concluded elections to the Lok Sabha. This was exploited by the Maoists.

Although the security forces have succeeded in ejecting the Maoists and their supporters from many of the villages earlier controlled by them, the fire is burning from inside.

Since Dr. Manmohan Singh came to power as the Prime Minister in 2004, he and his government have been projecting the Maoists as the greatest internal security threat faced by India and calling for and promising a special strategy to counter them through coordinated action involving the Centre and States in whose territory the Maoists are active. The Congress had appointed in 2004 a special task force of the party to go into the Maoist activities in Congress-ruled Andhra Pradesh to come out with suitable recommendations for dealing with the Maoist activities.

Before evolving a strategy, however, one has to understand the basic differences between Maoist insurgency/terrorism and jihadi terrorism. Firstly, the Maoist terrorism is an almost totally rural phenomenon, whereas jihadi terrorism is a largely urban phenomenon. Secondly, Maoist terrorism is a totally indigenous phenomenon motivated by domestic grievances and a domestic political agenda. Jihadi terrorism is externally sponsored or aided by the intelligence agencies of Pakistan and Bangladesh and is motivated by their strategic agenda. Jihadi terrorism is a cross border threat to national security. Maoist terrorism is not.

While the Maoist leaders are motivated largely by their desire to seek political power through a Maoist style People's War similar to the war waged by their counterparts in Nepal, their cadres and foot soldiers fighting for them are largely motivated by genuine grievances arising from the political, economic and social hardships.

It is India's long neglect to develop the tribal areas which has created large pockets of alienation against the government and these pockets have become the spawning ground of Maoist terrorism. The governments concerned have to take note of the genuine grievances of the tribals and deal with them in a sympathetic manner. There has to be a system for a prompt enquiry into all allegations of excess.

Also, Maoist terrorism cannot be effectively countered without modernising and strengthening our rural policing and the rural presence of the intelligence agencies. The tribal areas, which have not yet been affected by the Maoist virus, have to be developed on a crash basis in order to prevent the spread of the virus to them.

The capabilities of the security agencies deployed for countering Maoist activities also have to be different from those of the urban counter-terrorism agencies. The emphasis has to be on greater mobility in the rural areas and greater protection from land-mines used extensively by the Maoists. The failure to develop the road infrastructure in the rural areas has facilitated the spread of Maoist terrorism.

Maoists mainly attack police stations, police lines, camps and arms storage depots of para-military forces in order to demoralise the security forces and capture their arms and ammunition. The repeated success of the Maoists in mounting large-scale surprise attacks on such hard targets speaks of the poor state of rural policing and intelligence set-up and the equally poor state of physical security.

Unfortunately, instead of working out an appropriate strategy which will address these operational deficiencies and at the same time pay equal attention to the political handling of the problem, there is an unwise tendency to militarise the counter-Maoist insurgency management.

Bandopadhyay Committee

In May 2006, the Planning Commission appointed an expert committee headed by D. Bandopadhyay, a retired IAS officer instrumental in dealing with the Naxalites in West Bengal in the 1970s. The expert committee has underscored the social, political, economic and cultural discrimination faced by the SCs/STs across the country as a key factor in drawing large number of discontented people towards the Naxalites. The committee established the lack of empowerment of local communities as the main reason for the spread of the Naxal movement. Choosing its words carefully, the report states that "We have two worlds of education, two worlds of health, two worlds of transport and two worlds of housing.

The expert committee delved deep into the new conflict zones of India, i.e. the mines and mineral rich areas, steel zones, as well as the SEZs. The report holds the faulty system of land acquisition and a non-existent R&R Policy largely responsible for the support enjoyed by the Naxalites. On the other hand, the committee makes a forceful plea for a policy and legal framework to enable small and marginal farmers to lease-in land with secure rights while landless poor occupying government land should not be treated as encroachers.

For the first time in the history of the Naxal movement, a government appointed committee has put the blame on the State for the growth of the movement. Providing statistics of 125 districts from the Naxal-affected States, the committee finds out that the state bureaucracy has pitiably failed in delivering good governance in these areas. The report recommends rigorous training for the police force, not only on humane tactics of controlling rural violence but also on the constitutional obligation of the State for the protection of fundamental rights.

Making a departure from the usual government position, the expert committee concludes that development paradigm pursued since independence has aggravated the prevailing discontent among the marginalized sections of society. Citing democratic principles, the report also argues for the right to protest and discovers that unrest is often the only thing that actually puts pressure on the government to make things work and for the government to live up to its own promises. Dealing with Naxalism needs a holistic approach with development initiatives as an integral part of the security approach. Security here must be understood in its broader perspective, which includes human development in its scope, because human security is an inseparable component of any human development formula, and vice versa.

PLAN FOR NAXAL-HIT STATES

The Union Home Ministry has unveiled a new Rs. 500-crore fully Centre-sponsored scheme which will be implemented by State governments—for Naxalism-hit States. Centre will give Rs. 135-crore a year to the States under the scheme. The scheme has five important objectives: To provide mobility to the police by upgrading existing roads in inaccessible areas; to build camping grounds and helipads at strategic locations in remote areas; to strengthen police stations that have been identified as being at risk; to upgrade and strengthen approach roads to police stations and outposts where there is risk of IEDs and landmines, and to provide for critical needs, specific to the areas where holistic anti-naxal measures are being taken in a focused manner.

The States have been asked to prepare integrated action plans in the most affected districts to achieve the objectives. For this, the ministry has identified 15 action points that include preparation of a comprehensive connectivity plan for the 33 districts seriously affected by Left-wing extremism.

HOME MINISTER ADMITS TO GOVERNMENT LEVEL FAILURE

Alarmed by the apparent failure of the State machinery to tackle Naxalites, Union Home Minister P. Chidambaram admitted on July 15, 2009 that the government had failed in curbing Naxal menace in the country. Speaking in Rajya Sabha, Mr Chidambaram said the government had failed in assessing the threat posed by the Maoists, adding it also failed to tackle them with the seriousness they deserve. "Today they (Naxalites) pose a grave challenge ... We are preparing to take on the challenge. Details cannot be disclosed now," he said.

> "Regrettably for many years we did not properly assess the threat posed by Left-wing extremism. We under-estimated the challenge and in the meanwhile they (Naxalites) extended their influence," he added.

Chidambaram further informed that a military advisor has been appointed to prepare an action plan for dealing with Maoists. The Home Minister said he was in close touch with Chief Ministers of the Naxal-affected States and would hold a meeting with them to discuss ways to counter Left-wing extremism.

One could take a cue from the successful land reforms in Kerala, and to some extent West Bengal, that have not only assuaged agrarian tension, but have also undermined the clutch of ultras, while exactly to the contrary, failure of the same in Andhra Pradesh, Bihar and Chhattisgarh has changed what was essentially peasant struggle into Naxalite movements. A lasting solution to Left extremist politics cannot be achieved without addressing the socio-economic factors that contribute to its rise and growth.

Glossary

Alchiki : The language spoken by the Santhal tribe in Orissa.
Arhar : Type of pulse
Ayurveda : Indigenous Indian system of medicine.
Baba : Hindi term for holy man.
Bada dukh : Term for leprosy among the Bhil tribe in Madhya Pradesh.
Badvi : Term for magic among the Bhil tribe in Madhya Pradesh.
Bahariya : Tribal group in Madhya Pradesh.
Bajra : A coarse grain used for preparing unleavened bread in North India.
Bai : Term referring to arthritis-like conditions among the Sahariyas.
Baiga : Tribal group in Madhya Pradesh.
Ban-ruff : Term referring to conditions like eczema and scabies among the Sahariyas in Madhya Pradesh.
Banda : Generic term for scars and numbness used by some Sahariyas in Guna district of Madhya Pradesh.
Bengali doctor : Generic term referring to unregistered medical practitioner or quack.
Bhajan : Hindi term for singing religious hymns in a group.
Bhatudi : Tribe in Orissa.
Bhil : Tribe in Madhya Pradesh, Rajasthan and Gujarat. Meena Tribe predominantly living in Madhya Pradesh and Rajasthan.
Bhottada : Tribe in Orissa.

Bhuyan : Tribe in Orissa.
Chazon : Term for itching among the Sahariyas.
Chhau nritiya : Traditional folk dance in Orissa and Bengal.
Desari : Term for traditional healer among tribes in Mayurbhanj district in Orissa. Towards Leprosy Elimination in Tribal 108 ibal Communities
Desi : Generic adjective in Hindi meaning pure.
Dhruva : Tribe of Bastar district in Chhattsigarh.
Dongaria : Kondh Tribe in Orissa.
Gadaba : Dravidian language spoken by a tribe of the same name in Northeast India.
Ganda : Tribe of Orissa.
Gayatri Pariwar : Hindu socio-religious organisation working in the areas of health education and environment, mainly in North India.
Gayatri Yagnya : Prayers of the Gayatri Pariwar.
Gond : Tribe found in several parts of Central, West and South India.
Gram : Type of pulse.
Gram panchayat : Village-level tier of the three-tier panchayati raj system.
Gujar : Landowning caste in North India.
Gunia : Term for traditional healer among many tribal groups.
Haat : Hindi term for temporary market.
Halba : Tribe in Madhya Pradesh.
Jadi : butti Herbal treatment.
Jan Swasthy : Health worker trained to provide basic health services in
Rakshak : villages under an integrated rural health scheme of the Government of Madhya Pradesh.
Janpad Panchayat : The block-level tier of the PRI system.
Jowar : A course grain consumed in North India.
Juang : Language spoken by some tribal groups in Orissa.
Jan Parishad : Block-level tier of the panchayati raj system.
Jan Sahayak : People's leader or adviser.
Janbhagidari : Hindi term for people's participation.
Kala jatha : Term for street theatre group in Chhattisgarh.
Kala pathak : Term for street theatre in Madhya Pradesh.
Kanar : Tribe in Madhya Pradesh.
Kandla : Tribe in Orissa.

Khasi : Tribe in Northeast India.
Kisan : Tribe in Orissa.
Kirtan : Hindi term for religious prayers.
Kol : Tribe in Madhya Pradesh.
Kolam : Tribe in Andhra Pradesh and Maharashtra.
Kolha : Tribe in Orissa.
Korku : Tribe concentrated in Central and Western India.
Korh/kodh : Generic Hindi term referring to different types of skin problems ranging from copper-coloured patches of leprosy to leucoderma. It is also used derogatorily.
Korh vaabi : Term for leprosy among the Bhils in Madhya Pradesh.
Kotwar : Watchman.
Kotwar Munadi : Munadi is a traditional drum beaten by the kotwar to draw people's attention to any announcement to the village.
Krushnaprasad : SAPEL project in Puri district of Orissa.
Kukara bai : Term for deformity in hands and feet among the Sahariyas.
Kushta : Originally an ayurvedic classification of skin afflictions including leprosy.
Lodha : Tribal group in Orissa.
Mahila mandal : Women's group.
Mahua leaves : Plant used for preparing liquor.
Mela Madai : Term for market among the Gonds in Madhya Pradesh.
Motali Mata : Term for leprosy among the Bhils in Madhya Pradesh.
Mukhia : Traditional village leader.
Munda : Tribe in Northeast India.
Muria : Tribe of Bastar district in Chhattisgarh.
Nukad natak : Street Theatre.
Naxalite : A Marxist-inspired social movement with its base in Northeast and Central India.
Oroan : Tribe in Madhya Pradesh.
Palli sabha : Committee constituted at village-level for dealing with financial matters in Orissa.
Panch : Elected member of the panchayat.
Panchayat : Elected assembly, e.g., a village council.

Panchayati raj : Three tier system of local government in rural India. institution

Panchayat samiti : Committee constituted by panchayat, e.g. swasthya samiti (health committee).

Patbala : Term for leprosy among the Bhils in Madhya Pradesh.

Panch Prayas : Term used in Chhattisgarh to describe the active role of the PRI in leprosy elimination. Towards Leprosy Elimination in Tribal 110 ibal Communities

Paraja : Tribe in Orissa.

Project Bastaner : SAPEL project in Bastar district of Chhattisgarh.

Project Guru : SAPEL Project in Durg district of Chhattisgarh.

Project Lanji : SAPEL project in Lanji block of Balaghat district in Madhya Pradesh.

Project Gulaimal : SAPEL project in Khalwa block of Khandwa district in Project Madhya Pradesh.

Project Kolli Hills : SAPEL project in Namakkal district of Tamil Nadu.

Puja : Religious service.

Sabar : Tribe in Orissa.

Sachiv : Secretary.

Sahayek : Adviser or counsellor.

Sahariya : Tribe in Madhya Pradesh.

Sahariya Vikas : Government department responsible for welfare of the Adhikaran Sahariya tribe in Madhya Pradesh.

Sambhav : Gwalior-based NGO.

Santhal : Tribe in Orissa.

Saora : Tribe in Orissa.

Sarpanch : Elected chairman of the village panchayat.

Saura : Tribe in Madhya Pradesh.

Senjana Chaal : Medicinal plant used by the Sahariyas.

Sunnbai : Term for numbness in any part of the body among the Sahariyas.

Tendu leaves : Tobacco leaves.

Tribal hostels : Hostels of state-run boarding schools in tribal areas.

Tribal panchayat : Traditional system of self-government at village-level as different from the elected panchayat instituted within the framework of the panchayati raj institution.

Vaishno Mukti : Public functions organised by the Gayatri Pariwar in tribal Samroh areas to promote vegetarianism and discontinuation of liquor consumption among tribal communities.

Vimarsh : Bhopal-based NGO.

Yuva mandal : Youth group.

Zila Parishad : District-level tier of the panchayati raj system.

Index